Teaching Literature by Women Authors

by Carolyn Smith McGowen
with an introduction by Susan Moke

Clearinghouse on Reading
English, and Communication

IN COOPERATION WITH

CO-PUBLISHED 1993 BY
ERIC CLEARINGHOUSE ON READING, ENGLISH, AND COMMUNICATION
INDIANA UNIVERSITY
2805 EAST 10TH STREET, SUITE 150
BLOOMINGTON, INDIANA 47408-2698
CARL B. SMITH, DIRECTOR
AND
EDINFO PRESS
117 EAST SIXTH STREET
P.O. BOX 5247
BLOOMINGTON, INDIANA 47407

EDITOR: Warren Lewis
COVER DESIGN: David Smith
BOOK DESIGN: Lauren Bongiani Gottlieb and Theresa Hardy
PRODUCTION: Lauren Bongiani Gottlieb

ERIC (an acronym for **E**ducational **R**esources **I**nformation **C**enter) is a national network of 16 clearinghouses, each of which is responsible for building the ERIC database by identifying and abstracting various educational resources, including research reports, curriculum guides, conference papers, journal articles, and government reports. The Clearinghouse on **R**eading, **E**nglish and **C**ommunication (ERIC/REC) collects educational information specifically related to reading, English, journalism, speech, and theater at all levels. ERIC/REC also covers interdisciplinary areas, such as media studies, reading and writing technology, mass communication, language arts, critical thinking, literature, and many aspects of literacy.

TRIED is an acronym for **T**eaching **R**esources **I**n the **E**RIC **D**atabase.

This publication was funded in part by the Office of Educational Research and Improvement, U.S. Department of Education, under contract no. RR93002011. Contractors undertaking such projects under government sponsorship are encouraged to express freely their judgment in professional and technical matters. Points of view or opinions, however, do not necessarily represent the official view or opinions of the Office of Educational Research and Improvement.

LIBRARY OF CONGRESS CATALOGING-IN-PUBLICATION DATA

McGowen, Carolyn Smith, 1954-
  Teaching literature by women authors / by Carolyn Smith McGowen ; with an introduction by Susan Moke.
    p.   cm.
  Includes bibliographical references.
  ISBN 0-927516-38-1
  1. American literature--Women authors--Study and teaching. 2. English literature--Women authors--Study and teaching. 3. Women and literature--Study and teaching. I. Title.
PS42.M34 1993
810.9'9287'07--dc20   93-34695
                                                                                                                CIP

ERIC/RCS Advisory Board Members

Elaine Aoki
Seattle Washington Public Schools

Joan Baker
Cleveland State University

Douglas Barnard
Mesa Arizona Public Schools

James Gaudino
Speech Communication Association

Joan Irwin
International Reading Association

Julie Jensen
University of Texas, Austin

Diane Lapp
San Diego State University

Charles Suhor
National Council of Teachers of English

Arnold Webb
Research for Better Schools

TABLE OF CONTENTS

TRIED SERIES INTRODUCTION BY CARL B. SMITH viii

USER'S GUIDE ix

INTRODUCTION x

ACTIVITIES CHART xii

TEACHING A "WOMEN IN LITERATURE" COURSE 1

GENDER EQUITY 4
    Brainwashed in the Nursery 5
    Family Structure 10
    Recognizing and Challenging Stereotypes 12
    Gendered Meaning of Words 15
    Boy Toys and Girl Toys? 17
    Gender on the Job 20
    The Linguistics of Genderism 24
    Genderism in Fairy Tales 28

NOVELS 30
    Louisa May Alcott: *Little Women* 31
    Harriette Arnow: *The Dollmaker* 33
    Margaret Atwood: *The Handmaid's Tale* 36
    Emily Brontë: *Wuthering Heights* 38
    Pearl S. Buck: *The Good Earth* 40
    George Eliot: *Middlemarch* 42
    Bette Green: *Summer of My German Soldier* 44
    Rosa Guy: *The Friends* 48
    Madeline L'Engle: *A Wrinkle in Time* 51
    Ursula Le Guin: *A Wizard of Earthsea* 54
    Ursula Le Guin: *A Wizard of Earthsea* 56
    Jean Marzollo: *Halfway Down Paddy Lane* 59

TABLE OF CONTENTS (CONTINUED)

    Jean Marzollo: *Halfway Down Paddy Lane* 62

    L. M. Montgomery: *Anne of Green Gables* 64

    L. M. Montgomery: *Anne of Green Gables* 68

    Toni Morrison: *Sula/Song of Solomon/Tar Baby* 71

    Marjorie Rawlings: *The Yearling* 74

    Sandra Scoppettone: *The Late Great Me* 78

    Mary Shelley: *Frankenstein* 80

    Harriet Beecher Stowe: *Uncle Tom's Cabin* 83

    Mildred Taylor: *Roll of Thunder, Hear My Cry* 90

    Anne Tyler: *Dinner at the Homesick Restaurant* 93

    Laura Ingalls Wilder: *Little House in the Big Woods* 96

    Laura Ingalls Wilder: *Little House in the Big Woods* 98

    Agatha Christie: *Murder Mysteries* 100

BIOGRAPHY AND AUTOBIOGRAPHY 103

    Anne Frank: *Diary of a Young Girl* 104

    Anne Frank: *Diary of a Young Girl* 106

    Helen Keller: *The Story of My Life* 110

    Helen Keller: *The Story of My Life* 114

    Jessie Redmon Fauset and Mary Roberts Rinehart: Biographical Data ... 119

SHORT STORIES 125

    Tony Cade Bambara: "My Man Bovanne" 126

    Willa Cather: "Paul's Case" 127

    Caroline Gordon: "A Last Day in the Field" 129

    Shirley Jackson: "The Lottery" 133

    Shirley Jackson: "The Lottery" 135

    Joyce Carol Oates: "How I Contemplated the World from the 143
    Detroit House of Correction and Began My Life Over Again"

    Eudora Welty: "A Visit to Charity" and "A Worn Path" 147

Table of Contents (continued)

Poetry 149

    Dorothy Aldis: Sweet Rhymes 150

    Maya Angelou: "Harlem Hopscotch" 153

    Emily Dickinson: "A Narrow Fellow in the Grass" 155

    Eve Merriam and Lilian Moore: Sharing Poetry with Students 158

    Anne Sexton: "The Fury of Overshoes" 161

    Anne Bradstreet: Colonial Poetry 164

    Lucille Clifton: "An Ordinary Woman" 167

    Julia Malott: The Meaning of Her Poems 172

    Lois Prante Stevens: "Our Root Cellar" 176

    Lois Prante Stevens: "The Peddler" 182

    Phillis Wheatley: Revolutionary War Era Poetry 187

Annotated Bibliography of Related Resources in the ERIC Database ... 191

Series Introduction

Dear Teacher,

In this age of the information explosion, we can easily feel overwhelmed by the enormity of material available to us. This is certainly true in the field of education. Theories and techniques (both new and recycled) compete for our attention daily. Yet the information piling up on our desks and in our minds is often useless precisely because of its enormous volume. How do we begin to sort out the bits and pieces that are interesting and useful to us?

The **TRIED** series can help. This series of teaching resources taps the rich collection of instructional techniques collected in the ERIC database. Focusing on specific topics and grade levels, these lesson outlines have been condensed and reorganized from their original sources to offer you a wide but manageable range of practical teaching suggestions, useful ideas, and classroom techniques. We encourage you to use the citations to refer to the sources in the ERIC database for more comprehensive presentations of the material outlined here.

Besides its role in developing the ERIC database, the ERIC Clearinghouse on Reading, English, and Communication is responsible for synthesizing and analyzing selected information from the database and making it available in printed form. To this end we have developed the **TRIED** series. The name **TRIED** reflects the fact that these ideas have been tried by other teachers and are here shared with you for your consideration. We hope that these teaching supplements will also serve as a guide or introduction to, or reacquaintance with, the ERIC system and the wealth of material available in this information age.

Carl B. Smith, Director
ERIC Clearinghouse on Reading,
English, and Communication

User's Guide

These alternatives to textbook teaching offer practical suggestions for addressing the works of women authors in the English/language-arts classroom at elementary, middle-school, and secondary levels. Although the needs of individual students may vary significantly, the strategies and guidelines presented in this **TRIED** volume are useful for helping students to develop language-arts skills.

An "Activities Chart" (pages xii-xiii) indicates the focus and types of activities (such as creative tasks, research, vocabulary development, etc.) found in the various chapters. An annotated bibliography at the end of the book contains references to additional sources, as well as a list of other resources in the ERIC database with which to develop an entire curriculum for teaching women authors.

These teaching ideas were first tried and tested in the classroom environment, and then reported in the ERIC database. The ED numbers for sources in *Resources in Education* (RIE) are included to enable you to go directly to microfiche collections for the complete text, or to order the complete document from the ERIC Document Reproduction Service (EDRS). The citations to journal articles are from the *Current Index to Journals in Education*, and these articles can be acquired most economically from library collections or through interlibrary loan.

Beginning with the sources as found in the ERIC database, these strategies and approaches have been redesigned with a consistent format for your convenience. Each chapter includes the following sections:

>   **SOURCE** (your reference to the original in the ERIC database)
>   **BRIEF DESCRIPTION**
>   **OBJECTIVE**
>   **PROCEDURES**
>   **PERSONAL OBSERVATION**

The **TRIED** text is addressed to you, the teacher. In many instances, the text also addresses your students directly. These directions to the students are bulleted "✦". Read these instructions to your students, or revise them, as you prefer.

You know your students better than anyone else does. Adapt these suggestions to the ability levels present in your classroom. Some of the sources were written for specific levels, but they can be modified easily. Think of these chapters as recommendations from your colleagues who **TRIED** them and found that they worked well. Try them yourself, improve on them where you can, and trust your students to respond with enthusiasm.

INTRODUCTION

An unforgettable scene in Virginia Woolf's novel *To the Lighthouse* (1927) portrays a woman artist standing before her easel on the broad green lawn of a country house. Lily Briscoe is attempting to render her vision of a woman and child reading together in a window seat. An unremarkable, unmarried, nearly middle-aged woman, Lily is devoted to her few friendships and to nurturing her small talent. As she stands on the grass and struggles with the masses of color and form taking shape on her canvas, a male visitor to the country house comes up behind her and surveys her painting. After a moment or two, he pronounces his judgment by whispering these words in her ear: "Women can't paint. Women can't write." Lily is crushed, of course, and spends the rest of the novel turning this statement over in her mind, attempting to determine whether it is true. Virginia Woolf, a woman who began her writing career in the early part of the twentieth century, had often heard similar voices repeating the judgment that "women can't write." She describes such experiences as common to female authors of her era.

Most teachers of literature would not openly voice such a negative view of women's artistic potential, but it seems to me that every literature curriculum built around the traditional canon of largely male-authored texts sends students a similar message. Courses that require students to read few—if any—works by women writers let students know that women can't write well enough to be taken seriously. Fifteen or twenty years ago such courses were the norm in high-school and college classes. Now things are changing. The teaching resources in this **TRIED** reflect that change.

In the last two decades, feminist literary scholars have tackled the job of discovering and writing about a previously neglected body of work by women writers. The work of these scholars has enabled us to reclaim many powerfully insightful interpretations of women's experience from the dead-letter office of literary history. Collections such as Sandra Gilbert and Susan Gubar's *Norton Anthology of Literature by Women* (1985) demonstrate the rich variety of work created by women writers. This **TRIED** will help you and your students explore the abundant array of genres, plots, themes, and voices that make up the female literary tradition.

As you and your students take advantage of the resources provided here, questions about whether and how women's writing differs from men's will spark interesting debates in your classroom. Do women imagine specifically "feminine" stories? Widely accepted stereotypes about women's writing suggest that their work centers on domestic concerns and romantic relationships—on preoccupations with home and family—while the work of male authors typically traces the course of adventure and individual achievement. Taking a darker view, some literary critics suggest that women writers typically explore themes of confinement and escape. McGowen's book will help you and your students come to your own conclusions about the differences between the subjects, themes, and voices that predominate in men's and women's writing.

Not all the good ones are mentioned here. Should your class decide to explore the territory of romantic love as women writers have charted it, your journey could take you from the hostile and windy moors on which Heathcliff and Catherine's transcendent love took root, to the lush atmosphere of the Creole resort that serves as the backdrop for Kate Chopin's vivid dramatization of a woman's search for romantic love and personal freedom (*The Awakening*, 1899). If the turn of plots in Agatha Christie's murder mysteries suggest an interesting route of investigation for you and your students, you might "pry into" other female-authored whodunits such as playwright Susan Glaspell's bleak and intriguing drama, *Trifles* (1916) or Dorothy Sayer's captivating series of Lord Peter Whimsey mysteries.

Reading the African-American writers who are mentioned here—Toni Cade Bambara, Toni Morrison, Lucille Clifton, Phyllis Wheatley, and Mildred Taylor—may spark your interest in examining race and gender as they intersect in women's writing. If so, you will enjoy Zora Neale Hurston's lyrical and moving novel, *Their Eyes Were Watching God* (1937) and Alice Walker's *The Color Purple* (1982). The work of Native-American writers, Louise Erdrich (*Love Medicine,* 1984; *The Beet Queen,* 1986; *Tracks,* 1988; *The Crown of Columbus,* 1991) and Leslie Marmon Silko (*Ceremony,* 1977; *Storyteller,* 1981), traces the shadow of a lost past and offers a contemporary vision of what it means to be female and American Indian. Likewise, Chinese-American writers, Maxine Hong Kingston (*The Woman Warrior,* 1976; *China Men,* 1980) and Amy Tan (*The Joy Luck Club,* 1989; *The Kitchen God's Wife,* 1991), explore the female role as it is constructed in Chinese society. Chicana writer Sandra Cisneros (*The House on Mango Street,* 1985; *My Wicked Ways,* 1987) examines similar concerns from a different cultural perspective. Many routes are available to readers who choose to survey the varied topography of women's writing. The terrain may, at times, be difficult or painful or perhaps even disheartening at those moments when our deeply rooted beliefs about gender characteristics are challenged, but the journey itself will lead towards a deeper awareness of our culture and of our individual roles within it.

Literature gives us models to live by—it gives us new and imaginative ways to enlarge our understanding of our own emotions and experiences. Certainly your young women students will benefit from the strong female role models represented in the female literary tradition. But women's literature is not just for women. The teaching designs presented here will enable boys and girls alike to cultivate a more balanced view of themselves, of one another, and of the world in which they live.

—Susan Moke

Activities Chart

Novels	Creative Tasks	Research	Vocabulary Development	Writing Skills	Oral Reading	Drama/Role Play	Clustering	Journal Writing	Biographical Study	Probe Questions	Symbols	Compare/Contrast	Simulation
Louisa May Alcott (p. 31)	✓			✓	✓	✓		✓					
Harriette Arnow (p. 33)	✓			✓									
Margaret Atwood (p. 36)									✓	✓			
Emily Brontë (p. 38)	✓	✓							✓	✓			
Pearl S. Buck (p. 40)				✓		✓							
George Eliot (p. 42)		✓		✓			✓						
Bette Green (p. 44)				✓		✓							
Rosa Guy (p. 48)	✓			✓		✓		✓					
Madeline L'Engle (p. 51)				✓	✓		✓	✓					
Ursula Le Guin (p. 54)	✓												
Ursula Le Guin (p. 56)		✓							✓	✓			
Jean Marzollo (p. 59)				✓				✓			✓		
Jean Marzollo (p. 62)								✓					
L. M. Montgomery (p. 64)								✓					
L. M. Montgomery (p. 68)	✓				✓			✓					
Toni Morrison (p. 71)		✓	✓					✓					
Marjorie Rawlings (p. 74)		✓	✓					✓					
Sandra Scoppettone (p. 78)				✓								✓	
Mary Shelley (p. 80)		✓	✓					✓					
Harriett Beecher Stowe (p. 83)		✓				✓							✓
Mildred Taylor (p. 90)				✓		✓							
Anne Tyler (p. 93)				✓									
Laura Ingalls Wilder (p. 96)		✓	✓										✓
Laura Ingalls Wilder (p. 98)	✓	✓	✓							✓		✓	
Agatha Christie (p. 100)			✓										

Activities Chart (continued)

	Creative Tasks	Research	Vocabulary Development	Writing Skills	Oral Reading	Drama/Role Play	Clustering	Journal Writing	Biographical Study	Probe Questions	Symbols	Compare/Contrast	Simulation
Biography and Autobiography													
Anne Frank (p. 104)				✓			✓	✓					
Anne Frank (p. 106)				✓			✓	✓	✓				
Helen Keller (p. 110)	✓			✓	✓	✓		✓	✓				
Helen Keller (p. 114)								✓	✓				
Fauset/Rinehart (p. 119)	✓	✓			✓			✓	✓				
Short Stories													
Toni Cade Bambara (p. 126)				✓			✓						
Willa Cather (p. 127)				✓			✓						
Caroline Gordon (p. 129)				✓									
Shirley Jackson (p. 133)				✓			✓						
Shirley Jackson (p. 135)				✓						✓			
Joyce Carol Oates (p. 143)		✓		✓						✓			
Eudora Welty (p. 147)				✓									
Poetry													
Dorothy Aldis (p. 150)	✓		✓	✓					✓				
Maya Angelou (p. 153)	✓				✓						✓		
Emily Dickinson (p. 155)			✓	✓					✓				
Merriam/Moore (p. 158)	✓			✓	✓		✓		✓				
Anne Sexton (p. 161)				✓					✓				
Anne Bradstreet (p. 164)		✓		✓				✓	✓			✓	
Lucille Clifton (p. 167)								✓		✓		✓	
Julia Malott (p. 172)									✓	✓			
Lois Prante Stevens (p. 176)			✓	✓	✓								
Lois Prante Stevens (p. 182)			✓						✓				
Phillis Wheatley (p. 187)		✓		✓				✓					

Gender Equity

Teaching a "Women in Literature" Course

Source

Montgomery, Margaret D. "The Value of Their Lives," *English Journal*, v74 n3 March 1985, pp. 63-64.

Brief Description

Encourages students to explore one writer in depth; gives them an opportunity to write about their own lives, experiences, and feelings; provides a forum for the exchange of those ideas and feelings.

Objective

To acquaint students with the literature of women writers whose work enriches our literary heritage.

Procedures

Begin by asking your students to complete a questionnaire through which they investigate their pasts, assess their current awareness of themselves as women and men, and help themselves to see where they are headed.

Past

1. Which nationalities and ethnicities are up in your family tree?
2. Do you know when any of your ancestors came to America?
3. Where were you born?

Present

4. What courses are you taking in school?
   Is this course of study typical of males, females, or both?
5. What are your hobbies?
   Are these hobbies typical of males, females, or both?

6. Do you have a part-time job?
   If so, where? Is this job typical of males, females, or both?

FUTURE

7. Do you plan to go to college or university?
   If so, do you know where? Is it a coed school?

8. What vocation would you like to follow when you complete school?
   Is this vocation typical of males, females, or both?

9. Do you envision yourself as married? With children?

Compile the data from the questionnaires and share the general trends with the class.

Distribute a list of women authors to the class. Some authors that you might include in your list are these:

Louisa May Alcott	Susan Griffin
Maya Angelou	Shirley Jackson
Jane Austin	Fanny Kemble
Charlotte Brontë	Ursula Le Guin
Emily Brontë	Doris Lessing
Elizabeth Barrett Browning	Phyllis McGinley
Willa Cather	Toni Morrison
Emily Dickinson	Joyce Carol Oates
George Eliot	Sylvia Plath
Nora Ephron	Katherine Anne Porter
Anne Frank	Anne Tyler
Mary Wilkins Freeman	Alice Walker
Alice Gerstenberg	Jessamyn West
Charlotte Perkins Gilman	Laura Ingalls Wilder

Virginia Woolf

Lead a discussion about the number of authors that your students have heard of, which ones they are familiar with, and what they know about them.

Ask each student to select one writer as an independent focus for the course and learn as much as possible about her by reading biographical material, several representative works, and critical comments. Ask your students to prepare written summaries of their writers' achievements. Ask them as well to summarize what they have read, centering on how women are portrayed in the works; detailing the roles they play as daughters, sisters, friends, mates, etc; and discussing how much power these women have over their own lives and the lives of others. Finally, all students are to give brief talks about their authors to the rest of the class.

Two good volumes to use as bases for your literature discussion are *By Women: An Anthology of Literature* (Houghton Mifflin, 1976) and *The Norton Anthology of Literature by Women* (1985). Using these anthologies, you can examine a wide variety of selections and organize them in such a way as to trace the stages in a woman's life from childhood through maturity to old age and death.

For instance, you could begin with "Portrait of Girl with Comic Book" by Phyllis McGinley. *The Diary of a Young Girl* by Anne Frank may be used to contemplate a girl's entrance into womanhood. Katherine Anne Porter's "The Jilting of Granny Weatherall" shows the frustration of old age. You may want to complete your literature discussion with "A Wish" by Fanny Kemble ("...let fame/Over my tomb spread immortality!").

Throughout the course, encourage your students to keep journals wherein they comment on their reactions to each selection as a piece of literature, on its stirring their memories, and the feelings it evokes.

COMMENTS

Encourage your students to discuss their observations especially with their mothers, sisters, female friends, aunts, and grandmothers. You might invite local women writers to visit the class and share their experiences, struggles, and victories. This course can help students—boys and girls alike—to raise their expectations of themselves, value their own lives more, and honor the women of the past, while becoming themselves more literate.

Gender Equity

George Eliot

Gender Equity

Brainwashed in the Nursery

Source

Women's Studies: A Resource Guide for Teachers. British Columbia Department of Education, Victoria. January 1981. 97 pp. **ED 222 426**.

Brief Description

Students read a role-reversal story, participate in class discussion, write papers, evaluate family relationships, and recite rhymes.

Objectives

Students become aware of ways that gender roles are acquired as children grow up. They think about their own development and the influence of gender-role expectations.

Procedures

1. **Going on a role-reversal picnic**

    + Read the following role-reversal story, "The Picnic," designed to point out how males and females are brought up differently by being treated differently, often in ways of which we are not aware. Discuss the following questions:
        - What was your response to the story? Why?
        - What do you consider to be the main point of the story?

2. **Think about it!**

    Ask your students to write about their own experiences in learning gender roles. In what ways can they remember being treated as a female or a male? Have them include different areas of life (sports, dress, etiquette, fighting, crying, curfew rules) and different institutions (family, school, peers, church). Have your class share their experiences.

    Ask your students to examine the ways their parents treat them differently from their brother/sister. If students do not have a sibling of the opposite gender, have them examine a friend's parents' differing treatment of a male or female offspring.

The Picnic

Shawn got out of bed and drew back the pretty flowered curtains in his dainty pink and white bedroom. It was a brilliant sunny morning, and he giggled happily as he remembered the family picnic planned for the afternoon. He opened the closet and fingered the gaily colored T-shirts hanging there. First he took out the blue one, then the green one, but he couldn't decide which looked nicer.

"Daddy," he caroled down the stairway, "which T-shirt shall I wear?"

"I think the blue one looks nice because it goes with your eyes," Dad called back, "but put on an apron because I want you to help me this morning getting the food ready for the picnic."

Sharon tumbled sleepily out of bed and threw open the blinds. The sunlight streamed in, lighting up her new train set on the floor and the stamp collection on her desk. She hastily threw on her jeans, and yelled, "Is breakfast ready, Dad?" as she ran down the stairs.

"Yes, but come and eat quickly; your Mom wants you to help her get the barbecue ready, and hunt out the ball and net for the picnic."

Mom was already outside cleaning the car. "Hi honey," she said. "Why don't you go get the grill and the charcoal, and put them in the car? You're getting pretty strong now, so you should manage on your own." Mom whistled as she finished polishing the hood. "Sharon, why don't you check the tire pressure for me while I go get some coffee?" she added, striding off to the kitchen to see if the coffee were ready.

Dad and Shawn had nearly finished packing the picnic basket with bread and butter, cookies, and wieners. "Can I pour the coffee in the thermos, Dad?" asked Shawn.

"No," said Dad, "That coffee pot is very heavy, and I'm afraid you might spill it and scald yourself, but you can carry this mug of coffee over to your mother."

Mom sat in her special chair and looked happily around the kitchen which Dad always kept so clean and sparkling. She felt pleased to be able to sit and relax at home after she had worked so hard all week at the sawmill.

After lunch they all climbed into the car, and Mom drove down to the beach park. Sharon and Mom carried the things to a warm sheltered spot behind a big log, and Dad spread out the rugs to sit on.

Then he put on a big floppy hat and settled down with his crochet work.

"Let's play some ball, Mom," said Sharon.

"OK," said Mom. "We'll set up the net and have a game."

"May I play, too?" cried Shawn.

"Sure," said Mom, "You may play with us. Sharon, don't hit the ball too hard when you're sending it to Shawn."

They played for a little while, and then Dad called, "Shawn, you'd better stop playing now. You're getting too hot. Come and sit here with me for a while and wind this yarn for me."

Mom and Sharon played some more; then Mom flung herself down on the sand and said, "Whew, I'm tired! Why don't you kids go explore the beach?" She chucked Dad under the chin, "You look so cool and pretty, dear. I'll just lie here and rest by you while the kids go off."

Sharon and Shawn decided they would see how far they could go along the driftwood logs without touching the ground. They ran along and jumped from log to log, with Sharon helping Shawn when she thought it seemed too far for him to jump. Then they stopped where there was a big pile of driftwood, and they started to build a hut.

Suddenly Shawn screamed loudly, "A snake!" and ran to Sharon, who put her arm around him comfortingly. She took hold of a big stick and went over to where Shawn was pointing. Then she dropped the stick and shouted, laughing, "Oh Shawn, you are silly! It's just a piece of dried up old seaweed."

"Oh," said Shawn in a small voice, going pink. "Let's go back and have our picnic."

As they started back toward the park, they suddenly realized that the sea, which had seemed so far away before, now covered the whole beach. It was lapping right up against the cliff on the little headland they had walked around less than an hour before.

"Oh dear," said Shawn in a scared voice, "we've been cut off by the tide. Whatever shall we do?"

Sharon took his hand, and they climbed up onto a little ledge just underneath the cliff. "Look, there's a woman in a boat out there fishing. Let's shout for help," said Sharon.

So they both shouted as loudly as they could, "Help! Help! We are cut off by the tide." But the sound of the sea and the wind drowned their voices, and no one came to rescue them. By now, Shawn was really scared and was crying quietly.

"Never mind," said Sharon. "You wait here, and I'll go and get help."

"How?" asked Shawn.

"I'll climb the cliff and go and fetch Mom," said Sharon. She took off her sweater and made a little cushion so Shawn could be comfortable while he was waiting. Then she took a deep breath and started up the cliff. She pulled and pushed herself up, using crevices and jutting ledges and roots of small bushes as toe and finger holds. Near the top, her foot slipped, and Shawn held his breath anxiously as she swung by her hands for a moment from an overhanging rock. Then with a big effort, she swung herself up and disappeared over the edge of the cliff.

Shawn sighed with relief, settling himself down to wait patiently. He was a little nervous all by himself; he thought longingly of Georgie, his warm, cuddly, favorite doll.

Soon he heard a shout from above, and Mom's face appeared over the edge of the cliff. "We'll soon get you out of there," she called.

"Can I climb up, now?" cried Shawn, jumping up.

"No, no!" yelled Mom, "You're not strong enough to climb the cliff. The Coast Guard is coming to get you in her boat."

Sure enough, Shawn heard the chugging of a boat's engine, and soon the Coast Guard had brought her boat up to the side of the ledge where Shawn was marooned.

"You'll have to jump," she called to Shawn.

Shawn looked at the boat bobbing up and down in the water and cried, "I can't. I'm scared."

"It's OK," said the Coast Guard. "I'll catch you."

Shawn rolled up his pants, and, closing his eyes, jumped into the boat.

"I'll have you safe," said the Coast Guard, holding him gently in her strong brown arms, and she put him on the seat at the back of the boat. Then they chugged off around the headland, and soon Shawn was safely back at the picnic site.

"My, it's good to have you back safely," said Dad, hugging him.

"Yes, and we are certainly proud of Sharon," said Mom, clapping her firmly on the shoulder. "Now, let's have our picnic."

Mom and Sharon lit the barbecue coals and roasted the wieners, and Dad and Shawn set out the plates and cups and bread and cookies. When they had all eaten enough, they packed everything away, and Mom drove back home through the growing dusk.

"My, it was an exciting day," said Shawn as they climbed up to their rooms.

"Right on," said Sharon, and tumbled into bed to spend the night dreaming about joining the Coast Guard and rescuing boys trapped on ledges.

~ ~ ~

3. Sex, Lies, and Nursery Rhymes

Discuss the following rhymes in class:

> What are little girls made of?
> Sugar and spice
> And everything nice.
> That's what little girls are made of.

> What are little boys made of?
> Snakes and snails
> And puppy dogs' tails.
> That's what little boys are made of.

Reflecting on "The Picnic" and your students' own experiences, ask them to write some alternative, non-sexist ingredients of which little boys and little girls may be made.

Ask them to turn their list of ingredients into a four-line poem that rhymes ABBA.

Enjoy a "poetry reading" as everyone takes turns reading their rhymes to the class. (You write one, too, teacher, and read it.)

Family Structure

Source

Women's Studies: A Resource Guide for Teachers. British Columbia Department of Education, Victoria. January 1981. 97 pp. **ED 222 426**.

Brief Description

Students examine their family members' roles by making lists and charts, analyzing their results, examining television shows, and doing a detailed study.

Objectives

Students come to understand the influence of the family in defining gender roles.

Procedures

Have each student analyze the division of labor in his or her own family or in a family with which he or she is familiar, whether through TV, movies, books, or personal acquaintance. Make a list of activities (doing dishes, shopping, earning income, fixing the leaky tap, disciplining the children, changing diapers, etc.) and note how often each member of the family performs them.

Now have your students analyze the division of power and authority in a variety of areas. For example, who makes consumer decisions and decisions about leisure-time activities, the activities of children, the use of family resources (who gets the car, etc.)? What patterns emerge? Who tells whom what? How can you explain variations?

Ask your students to examine the ways in which families are portrayed on a variety of television shows: family sitcoms, *Masterpiece Theatre, The Cosby Show, Married with Children*, soaps (daytime and nighttime), and others. What roles do the women play in each family? How realistic are the family situations?

Ask your students to write a scene in which one of these families deals with the man's or woman's decision to change his or her role.

Ask your students to do "a day in the life of..." study. Look at individual family members and their daily activities. Learn in detail what men and women in families do. How do male and female children differ in their activities?

TEACHING LITERATURE BY WOMEN AUTHORS

Recognizing and Challenging Stereotypes

Source

Equity Lessons for Secondary School. Philadelphia School District, Pennsylvania Office of Curriculum and Instruction. 1982. 65pp. **ED 223 510**

Brief Description

Students find word definitions, participate in class discussions, complete a checklist, write a paragraph, keep an observation log, and participate in role-play exercises.

Objectives

Students understand what a gender stereotype is. They recognize the stereotypes they have about other people. They identify their own assumptions about what it means to be female or male. Through discussion with one another and observing the world about them, they challenge instances of stereotyping.

Procedures

1. **Defining and Discussing Stereotyping**

    Help your students arrive at a common understanding of the term "stereotype" first by finding the definition in a dictionary. Then encourage students to draw on their own experience and knowledge to elaborate the definition.

    Direct a group discussion in analyzing stereotypes with regard to gender, race, age, ethnicity, religion, class, physical disabilities, and other variables. You may want to use the following questions to discuss each variable.

    ◆ What words are often used to describe _____ people?

    ◆ What are some things people say about the ways that _____ people are?

- What personal experiences have you had that cause you to challenge the validity of these characterizations of _____ people?

- Do jobs have gender? What is "woman's work?" What is "man's work?"

2. **IDENTIFYING PERSONAL ASSUMPTIONS**

    Complete the "Assumptions" checklist on the next page.

    - Write a paragraph about what it means to you to be female or male. Consider the following ideas as you write:

        a. What do you like most/least about being female/male?

        b. How would your life be different if you were the other gender?

            1. Right now

            2. Ten years from now

        c. Would you rather have a brother or a sister? Why?

        d. What is a "sissy?" What is a "tomboy?" Which is worse to be? Why?

        e. What are the physical differences between men and women? Do the physical differences cause any other differences? Are there differences other than physical ones that make all women different from all men? Have these differences been the same since the beginning of time?

3. **OBSERVING GENDER-ROLE STEREOTYPES IN EVERYDAY LIFE**

    - For the next two weeks, keep a log of your observations of instances of gender-role stereotypes in everyday life (people you meet and know, television, newspaper or magazine articles, etc.). Record the comment heard or action observed, who was speaking or acting, to whom it was done, and a brief description of the context in which it happened.

    Ask your students to share and discuss their feelings and opinions based on their gender-stereotypes observation logs.

    Ask them to brainstorm and role-play various responses that might counteract the kinds of stereotypes that they recorded in their logs.

    Ask: "What could you say or do the next time you encounter a certain stereotypical remark or action directed at you or at someone else?"

    Encourage your students to challenge stereotypes by offering corrective information from their own experience, but not by "getting back" at the other person.

CHECKLIST: "IDENTIFYING YOUR ASSUMPTIONS"

Complete both columns, placing the letter G (for girls) and B (for boys) next to the items that apply to you.

(G) Because I am a girl, I would not: (G) *If* I were a boy, I would not:
(B) *If* I were a girl, I would not: (B) Because I am a boy, I would not:

____ wear curlers in front of a boy   ____ cook
____ dress like a man in a play   ____ knit
____ climb a tree   ____ wash dishes
____ climb a tree wearing a skirt   ____ help with housework
____ play baseball   ____ wear a dress in a play
____ beat a boy at a sport or game   ____ cry in public
____ try to join a boys' club or team ____ cry at a movie
____ hit a boy   ____ hit a girl
____ kiss my mother in public   ____ kiss my father in public
____ kiss my mother at all   ____ kiss my father at all
____ get into a fist fight   ____ wear beads or jewelry
____ get into a fist fight with a boy ____ babysit
____ get into a fist fight with a girl ____ back out of a fight
____ get a very short haircut   ____ hug a male friend
____ yell when I'm angry   ____ go grocery shopping
____ ride a skateboard   ____ wear pretty colors
____ go out to a movie by myself   ____ play a game with all girls
      on a weekend night

Fill in other items that may be missing from the list.

____   ____

____   ____

____   ____

____   ____

____   ____

____   ____

GENDERED MEANING OF WORDS

SOURCE

Austin, Kitty. *Incorporating the Multicultural, Nonsexist Guidelines into the Language Arts Curriculum. Grades 9-12.* Area Education Agency 7, Cedar Falls, Iowa. 1980. 79pp. **ED 241 926**

BRIEF DESCRIPTION

Students examine gender-related word meanings by grouping them, using them in sentences, identifying gender, and changing words in written pieces.

OBJECTIVES

To show the present state of confusion about word usage regarding males and females: Some usages refer to a male or a female, some to males and females, and some are ambiguous.

PROCEDURES

By having your students examine the following questions, show them that word usage can be confusing.

1. Do only babies have babysitters?
2. Do only ships take shipments?
3. Are only kids kidnapped?
4. Do you spend only dimes at a dimestore?
5. Do you stir only tea with teaspoons?
6. Are only white sheets sold at a white sale?
7. Are only men freshmen?
8. Do only fellows get fellowships?
9. Do only bachelors get bachelor's degrees?
10. Can only men get workmen's compensation?

✦ Collect examples of words that appear to be masculine gender, but can be used to refer to both male and female.

- ✦ Harder to do, collect examples of words that appear to be feminine gender, but can be used to refer to both male and female.

Have your students sort the examples into groups that actually refer to a male or a female, ones that clearly refer to both male and female, and ones that are ambiguous.

Now, ask your students to examine sentences that appear to have a specific gender direction, but actually apply to both genders.

1. "All men are created equal."*
2. "The best candidate will be hired regardless of his race, color, or sex."
3. "...with which the layman can diagnose her own pregnancy."
4. "Man, being a mammal, breast feeds his young."
5. "Man is the only primate that commits rape."

Another way to demonstrate this confusion is to pass out a list of words that contain a masculine marker, and then have your students circle the ones that they think could also refer to females. This list could include the following:

fireman	serviceman	postman	repairman
policeman	milkman	deliveryman	firstbaseman
freshman	gentleman	workmen	horseman
journeyman	brakeman	lineman	layman
mannish	penmanship	manslaughter	*human
menfolk	menswear	*mentor	manhandle
*manager	*mandate	maneater	manhole
manhour	manhunt	manly	mankind
mannequin	manmade	manpower	woman

The asterisked terms look as if they were etymologically gendered, but they are scattered throughout the list as word-tricks to be played on your students. A bit of dictionary work will dispel the appearance of gender.

Ask your students to compare their results. Some students will circle all the words, some only half, and some only a few or none.

Select a written piece that contains lots of "man" words in it. Ask the students to read the piece substituting "person" or "individual" or "human" or "one" for "man." The point is not necessarily to recommend this substitution in all cases. The purpose is to bring the potential for confusion to the students' attention and to make them aware of gender-exclusive language.

*Historical note: The Founding Fathers probably did not mean to say that "all people are created equal," and therefore they did not say it. Women, Black slaves, and Native Americans were originally excluded from the constitutional guarantees of democracy. Nowadays, however, most Americans see the matter differently.

Gender Equity

Boy Toys and Girl Toys?

Source

Equity Lessons for Elementary School. Philadelphia School District, Pennsylvania Office of Curriculum and Instruction. 1982. 42pp. **ED 223 509**

Brief Description

Students examine toys, answer questions, complete handouts, look at advertising and containers, and design a nonsexist wrapping or write a gender-inclusive ad.

Objectives

Students identify gender-role stereotypes on toy packaging and in toy advertising, and they make suggestions for improvement. They compose a nonsexist radio or television toy ad or toy packaging.

Procedures

Toys, Toys, Toys

1. As a class, make a list of toys that your students would like to receive as gifts. Discuss their choices.

    a. Why do you want it?

    b. What do you like about it?

    c. What makes you think this is a good toy for you?

    d. Where did you first find out about this toy?

2. You and your students gather a wide variety of toy packaging and magazine/newspaper ads for toys.

3. Distribute a *Toy Category Sheet* to each student. Have students complete the sheets.

    a. Into what category does this toy fit?

    b. Is the toy being "watched," "played with," or both?

    c. Who is using the toy (girl, boy, woman, man)?

d. Who else might enjoy this toy (that is, if a girl is pictured, might a boy enjoy it, and vice versa)?

e. Is the advertising or packaging aimed exclusively, or mainly, at females or males? Should it be? Why or why not?

f. Why do you think the manufacturer depicted the toy's being used in a certain way?

g. What changes do you think ought to be made?

3. Distribute a toy category sheet to each student. Have students complete the sheets. (See next page.)

4. Discuss each container and each ad.

5. Divide students into as many groups as there are categories on the *Toy Category Sheet*. Have each group fill out the *Toy Checklist* for its category, and then discuss their findings. Have students refer to the display of toy packaging and advertising.

    a. Which category(ies) featured the most girls?

    b. Which category(ies) featured the most boys?

    c. Were any categories equal?

6. Have your students design nonsexist packaging or write gender-inclusive ad copy for an existing or imagined toy. Have them work individually or in teams, and then share their work with the whole class.

Toy Checklist

Name of Toy	Total Number of Boys on Package	Number Playing	Number Watching	Total Number of Girls on Package	Number Playing	Number Watching

Toy Category Sheet

Game	Craft	Homemaking Toy	Sports Toy	Action Toy	Other

Gender on the Job

Source

Equity Lessons for Elementary School. Philadelphia School District, Pennsylvania Office of Curriculum and Instruction. 1982. 42pp. **ED 223 509**

Brief Description

Students examine pictures of men and women on the job, participate in class discussion, complete statements, compare words with similar meanings, define words, examine newspapers, and read a story.

Objectives

Students understand that job requirements, with extremely few exceptions, are unrelated to gender. They become able to recognize job discrimination by gender.

Procedures

Look at the Pictures

With your students, gather a collection of magazine and advertising pictures of people working. Some of them will be gender-stereotypical, such as a female homemaker or a male business executive.

Encourage your students to watch for pictures of men and women doing work that is non-stereotypical for their gender, such as the following:

- A female construction worker
- A male ballet dancer
- A female jockey
- A female racecar driver
- A male nurse
- A mother at work outside the home
- A father at work inside the home

Gender Equity

Talk about it. Raise the following questions for discussion:

a. Is there a gender difference in the ability to perform some jobs?

b. Should there be a difference in salary between women and men who perform the same job?

c. Is there a difference between "women's work" and "men's work?"

Distribute the "Think about it and then write about it" handout, and ask your students to write what they think.

THINK ABOUT IT AND THEN WRITE ABOUT IT.

a. It's a woman's responsibility to _____
_____
_____

b. Supporting one's family is a job for _____
_____
_____

c. Husbands who do housework are _____
_____
_____

d. Men who do not marry are _____
_____
_____

e. Women who do not marry are _____
_____
_____

f. _____ is woman's work because _____
_____
_____

g. _____ is man's work because _____
_____
_____

A Worker by Any Other Name . . .

Introduce the concept that an accurate job title best describes the work that is being done, rather than the gender of the person who is doing it.

Have your students complete the "job name" exercise (next page), matching each "old" job title on the left with the "new" title on the right.

Invite your students to list other gender-role stereotyped job titles, and replace them with new titles.

Examples:

garbageman: garbage collector, sanitation worker

dockman: dock worker

assemblyman: state legislator, representative

Genderism in the News

1. Display the front page of a local newspaper and the cover of a local magazine. Discuss the gender of the writers of the various articles. (Note: Most front-page news and "scoops" are still being written by men, whereas most fashion, advice, and lifestyle articles are still being written by women.)

2. Have your students analyze newspaper sections for articles traditionally written by men and traditionally written by women. Newspaper sections will include household hints, fashion, advice, sports, front-page news, editorial columns, major scoops, book reviews, interviews, food news, medical advice, and many others. Have your students analyze the placement of advertising in relation to the various sections.

3. Ask your students to read the story of Nellie Bly, a famous news reporter. Discuss the problems she had convincing editors to give her assignments besides fashion and food reporting. Do you think this problem is still encountered today?

4. Have students define, explain, and discuss the following words, using both a dictionary and their own knowledge and experience:

    a. sexism
    b. gender exclusivity
    c. female roles
    d. male roles
    e. gender stereotypes
    f. sexual equality
    g. gender discrimination
    h. folkways
    i. customs
    j. laws

Gender Equity

MATCH THE OLD JOB WITH THE GENDER-NEUTRAL NAME.

_____ foreman   a. waiter's assistant

_____ maid   b. fire fighter

_____ busboy   c. cleric

_____ airline stewardess   d. trash collector

_____ fireman   e. fisher

_____ clergyman   f. domestic worker

_____ policeman   g. shoe repairer

_____ laundress   h. supervisor

_____ shoe repairman   i. police officer

_____ trashman   j. laundry worker

_____ fisherman   k. flight attendant

TEACHING LITERATURE BY WOMEN AUTHORS

THE LINGUISTICS OF GENDERISM

SOURCE

Equity Lessons for Elementary School. Philadelphia School District, Pennsylvania Office of Curriculum and Instruction. 1982. 42pp. **ED 223 509**

BRIEF DESCRIPTION

Students design language charts using both sexist and nonsexist photographs and stories. They complete an attitude checklist and participate in class discussion.

OBJECTIVES

Students learn that our society—home, school, mass media—channels us into specified roles that do not always allow for the development of our individual human potential, regardless of one's gender. Your students develop the ability to recognize instances of stereotyping, with special reference to gender-role stereotypes.

PROCEDURES

THE GRAMMAR OF GENDER

You and your students gather a large collection of pictures of males and females doing things, performing gender-role related tasks. Have your students describe in their own words the people in the pictures in terms of the activities performed (reading, running, serving) and the personal characteristics of the people performing. Tell your students to trust their own perceptions and use any language they like (busy, energetic, rough) to describe the people and actions. Chart the responses in grammatical categories.

THE GRAMMAR OF GENDER

NOUNS	PRONOUNS	ADJECTIVES	VERBS
girl	she	pretty	sewing
man	he	big	hammering
woman	she	kind	helping
boy	he	rough	playing

Now, you and your students construct meaning from the evidence in the chart and pictures. What do women do? How do they do it? What do men do? How do they do it? Boys? Girls? What does all this tell us about gender stereotypes?

Ask your students to examine the chart, using gender as a reference point.

1. Which "action words" (verbs) belong to males in the pictures?
2. Which "description words" (adjectives) belong to males in the pictures?
3. Which "action words" (verbs) belong to females in the pictures?
4. Which "description words" (adjectives) belong to females?

Sort the picture gallery into two groups: one pile of pictures that your class agrees are more-or-less sexist in their gender-stereotypes, and the other pile of pictures that your students agree are mostly non-sexist and gender-inclusive.

Have each student choose a few photographs from either of the two collections. Selection could be made on the basis that the photographs most accurately reflect life as the student experiences it, or on the basis of an ideal to be achieved, or on some other basis. Have your students write stories about the people in their chosen pictures. Then, ask your students to trade stories, read one another's writings, and discuss implications.

THE LANGUAGE OF GENDER

Have your students complete the following sentences, and then discuss their reactions and the implications.

Girls can (cannot) _____.

All _____ are strong.

Men who do housework are _____.

Women who work outside the home are _____.

Women could never be _____.

_____ make better doctors.

_____ should never cry.

_____ like children more than _____.

1. Distribute an attitude checklist like the one below. Have students categorize each word as F for female, M for male, B for both, or N for neither.

____ cooking	____ brave	____ teacher	____ aggressive
____ running	____ smart	____ farmer	____ irresponsible
____ sewing	____ loving	____ baker	____ bullish
____ helping	____ gentle	____ engineer	____ gossipy
____ racing	____ selfish	____ politician	____ competent
____ watching	____ married	____ winner	____ athletic

2. Have students discuss their reactions, first in small groups and then as a class.

3. Have students take the checklist home for parents' and other relatives' responses. Discuss the results in class.

THE LITERATURE OF GENDER

1. Divide the class into groups. Have each group examine a story or other literary text. Ask them to chart their findings on the "Literature of Gender" chart.

THE LITERATURE OF GENDER

TITLE OF STORY
_____

NAME OF CHARACTER

	Child or Adult	Female or Male	Description of Character	Actions of Character

2. Discuss the findings of each group, using gender as a reference point.

   a. Which words are used for females?

   b. Which words are used for males?

   c. Are any words used for both females and males? How many times?

   d. Are similar words used for male children and male adults? For female children and female adults?

   e. Does this type of language use make us expect females and males to act in certain ways just because they are females and males?

TEACHING LITERATURE BY WOMEN AUTHORS

GENDERISM IN FAIRY TALES

SOURCE

Buckland, Freddie; and others. "Curriculum Units on Nonsexist Teaching." Colorado University, Boulder. *Women Studies Program*. 1983. 508pp.
ED 243 806

BRIEF DESCRIPTION

Students examine traditional fairy tales. They answer questions, define phrases, write a story, draw a picture, and complete a story.

OBJECTIVES

Students realize that female and male stereotypes are portrayed in most fairy tales.

PROCEDURE

1. Make a list of the class's favorite fairy tales.
   Read one of their favorites aloud to the class.

2. Ask your students the following questions:
   a. Who is your favorite character? Why?
   b. Which of the men (boys) or women (girls) in the story would you least like to be? Why?
      most like to be? Why?

3. Invite your students to speculate on whether the story (or some version of it) could happen in real life.*

4. Ask your students to tell what the following phrases mean to them:
   a. cruel stepmother
   b. wicked witch
   c. her knight in shining armor
   d. lived happily ever after

*Historical Note: Setting aside the magical qualities, very many fairy tales are stories about actual events that truly happened to real people.

e. the beautiful princess

f. the brave knight

Ask your students to name various fairy-tale characters evoked by these phrases.

Ask your students to write a story or draw a picture telling what they think life will be like for Cinderella, Snow White, or another fairy-tale character five years after the end of the story.

Invite your students to complete the following story:

> Once upon a time there was a brave princess. One day she was riding her horse through the forest when she saw a young prince riding toward her. Suddenly, a ferocious dragon jumped out from behind a large rock and knocked the prince off his horse. He was hurt badly and could not escape. The princess knew she had to save him, so she....

Have your students read and discuss one another's story endings in small groups.

After their small-group work, begin a class discussion of traditional fairy tales by asking the following questions:

1. Why doesn't the princess ever rescue the prince?
2. Can women be brave and strong?
3. What happens to men when they are in trouble?
4. What would happen to the princess if no one came to rescue her?
5. Why don't they ever feed a prince to the dragon?

Ask your students: "Does anyone know of any fairy tales that are not sexist?" If so, read them in class and discuss them.

NOVELS

Charlotte Brontë

LITTLE WOMEN
BY LOUISA MAY ALCOTT

SOURCE

Morris-Lipsman, Arlene J. *Notable Women: Grades 4-6*. Scott, Foresman and Company, Department GYB, 1900 East Lake Avenue, Glenview, IL 60025. 1990. 128 pp. **ED 331 737**

BRIEF DESCRIPTION

Students emphasize critical and innovative thinking skills involving written, oral, dramatic, and art projects.

OBJECTIVE

Encourages students to question and imagine the struggles of one of America's best-loved women authors.

PROCEDURES

By 1867, Louisa May Alcott was well-known to magazine editors and publishers. One of these publishers asked her to write a book for young girls. Louisa hesitated because she felt that she knew nothing about young girls. Eventually the publisher persuaded her to write. Considering what to write about, she realized that her own family was her best source. In 1868, the book *Little Women* was published.

ASSIGNMENT 1

Louisa May Alcott wrote books and stories for adults, but she is best-known for her children's books. Many of these books are based on Louisa's own experiences. Read her book *Little Women*.

- Imagine that you are Louisa and that you have been asked to write a children's story. First, skim through the first two chapters of *Little Women* to see how Louisa told her family's story. Now, think of a story to tell based on your own life. Because this is fiction, change the names of your characters (as Louisa did). You may want to change the names of places and some of the important details.

- Think about an event that happened in your own life; then write a story about this event. Include conversations between characters.

- Share your story with your classmates by reading it aloud.

Assignment 2

- When Louisa was a child, she wrote plays that she and her younger sisters acted out. Pretend that you are Louisa and write a play.

- Divide into small groups. Go to the library and obtain a biography of Louisa May Alcott. Think about the experiences of her life. Which ones seem the most exciting to you?

- Use one of these experiences and write a short play. Be sure to include parts for Louisa's family or people whom she met. As you write the speaking parts for the characters, try to imagine what they might actually have said and how they might have felt in the situation.

- Make paper-bag puppets for each character in your play. Draw faces and bodies on paper bags. Stuff the bags with newspaper and staple them together at the bottom. Attach a stick or ruler to the bottom of the bag in order to support the puppet. Use your paper-bag puppets as the Greeks used their theatrical masks: You, the actor, speak from behind the puppet/mask.

- Present your play to the rest of your classmates using the puppets to act it out.

Read about it!

- Louisa dreamed of being able to support her family. Her father, Bronson Alcott, a brilliant man, was unable to provide for his family. Find out more about Bronson Alcott, his unusual ideas, and how these ideas affected Louisa's early life.

- Find out how many other children's books Louisa wrote. What are the books about? Read some! Were they as popular as *Little Women*? Did you enjoy them as much?

The Dollmaker

by Harriette Arnow

Source

Brennan, Joan M. *Appalachian Literature and Culture: A Teaching Unit for High School Students.* 1981. 43 pp. **ED 209 048**

Brief Description

Students view a film on the people of Appalachia, prepare in-class presentations, and write short essays to explore the meaning of culture as expressed in film and text.

Objective

To encourage students to appreciate backgrounds different from their own.

Procedures

Introduce the subject of Appalachian life by showing a film that portrays the Appalachian people authentically. The source has a film bibliography, and a description of the geography, flora and fauna, and the history of Appalachia.

Assign the reading of Harriette Arnow's book, *The Dollmaker.*

Ask each student to prepare a presentation demonstrating one of the arts and crafts indigenous to the Appalachians. In giving their presentations, students will give the history, background, and other relevant information concerning the subject, stating their sources of information. If appropriate, students may collaborate. Many styles of presentations are possible, and variety is enjoyable:

1. ***Drama:*** Storytelling; tall tale; monologue such as "Brier's Sermon"; novel enacted, such as the dramatization of John Fox, Jr.'s work; or short stories improvised.

2. ***Music:*** Singing a ballad or folk tune; "show-and-tell" of instruments characteristic of Appalachia, such as the dulcimer, the banjo, and the Jew's harp.

3. ***Dance:*** Demonstrating country dancing or folk dancing; directing the other students in a square dance or reel, and sponsoring a square dance for the school.

4. ***Art:*** Visual arts; manual arts, such as ceramics and carving, sculpting or whittling; crafts, such as quilting, basketweaving, making corn-husk dolls or apple dolls; a pictorial essay on Appalachian culture for students of photography.

5. ***Research report:*** Consulting *The Reader's Guide to Periodical Literature,* the students could research a recent article appearing in a magazine or other periodical relating to contemporary events in the Appalachian region, and present the information to the class in an oral report.

After reading *The Dollmaker,* have your students write about the story, answering some or all of the the essay questions as their guide (see next page). Have various students read their "best answers," and invite a full-class discussion.

Novels

Answer the following questions as fully as possible. Support your opinions with examples from the text or give other evidence and reasons, as appropriate.

1. Did Gertie's mother give Gertie good advice when she urged Gertie to follow Clovis into the city instead of buying the Tipton place?

2. In what ways did Reuben share his mother's views? Be specific. Will Reuben be better off "back home" than if he had stayed in the city? Explain Gertie's reasons for reacting as she did when she learned where Reuben had gone.

3. Contrast Gertie's and Clovis's views on religion. Who, in your opinion, was the more "religious?" (Remember, reasons!)

4. Discuss what Gertie meant when she said, "I want 'em to be happy, but I don't know as I want 'em to...adjust."

5. Defend or debate the following statement: Clovis was, in many ways, selfish and immature.

6. Cite some of the degradations that Gertie's family has to endure in their new dwelling place.

7. What does the block of cherry wood symbolize in this story? Relate this to Gertie; to Cassie.

8. Knowing that Gertie considered her whittling of dolls to be "foolishness," and that she did not earn her livelihood by dollmaking, how would you justify the title of this novel, *The Dollmaker*?

9. Write a sequel to this story. Begin your episode ten years after the novel leaves off.

10. Write a well-developed character sketch, supporting the following theme:

    While fighting against nearly insuperable odds, Gertie proved to be a woman of strength, courage, and integrity.

THE HANDMAID'S TALE

BY MARGARET ATWOOD

SOURCE

Thomson, Susan Gotsch. "The Integration of Gender into Teaching of Classical Social Theory: Help from 'The Handmaid's Tale,'" *Teaching Sociology*, v18 n1 Jan 1990, pp. 69-73.

BRIEF DESCRIPTION

Students identify symbols that are central to the text, identify main ideas, and summarize them; they learn to recognize the link between fiction and reality.

OBJECTIVE

To understand the use of symbols in literature; to give students practice in oral communication and identifying main ideas.

PROCEDURE

Assign Margaret Atwood's book, *The Handmaid's Tale*, to your students to read. Explain to them that it is a story of women under the control of Gilead, a repressive religious regime set in the not-too-distant future in the United States. The story centers on the life of a woman used as a "birthing machine," and it richly describes her thoughts about herself and her life, the rituals of the regime, and the roles of women (and some men).

Divide the class into small groups of four or five students. Assign each group a chapter from the book.

- While reviewing your chapter, look for the symbols that are essential for individual survival in Gilead. One example is the phrase containing the word "Mayday" or *m'aidez*. This word was used as a password among those who opposed the regime.

- Are there symbols in today's society with similar meanings?

Maintaining the same groups, assign different discussion questions to each group. Ask each group to choose a recorder.

- Is Gilead characterized by mechanical or organic solidarity? Why?
- What are the rituals of the society, and how do they reinforce the values of the society?
- What are some of the sacred objects in this society, and what are the indicators of their sacredness?
- What kind of law is found in the society, and what does that indicate about other aspects of society?

Ask the recorders to report their groups' answers to the whole class, with full-class discussion to follow.

COMMENT

This book can be used to incorporate a gender perspective into the teaching of social theories.

Wuthering Heights
by Emily Brontë

Source

Gilliard, Fred. "British Writers: Modules for Teacher Corps." 1977. 23 pp. **ED 150 611**

Brief Description

Students review or learn literary terminology, do historical research, complete an inventive activity, and answer a set of questions as they read the novel.

Objective

To become acquainted with the development of the English novel; familiar with literary Romanticism; and able to recognize the functions of language, structure, and characters in literature.

Procedures

Refresh your own knowledge of the following literary terms so that you can discuss them with your students:

> English Novel
>
> Romanticism
>
> Neo-Classicism
>
> Narrator
>
> Gothic

Research the life of Emily Brontë, and prepare a brief history of England in her day.

Assign *Wuthering Heights* by Emily Brontë to your students.

Select one of the following activities:

- ✦ Draw a map of the general setting where the action occurs. Use colors to indicate the differences between various areas.

- Pick one member of the Linton family and one of the Earnshaw family and sketch them.

- Listen to a recording of Tchaikovsky's "Romeo and Juliet." Describe the mood it evokes as a complement to the mood in *Wuthering Heights*.

As your students reread the novel, have them answer the following questions:

- What do Mrs. Dean and Mr. Lockwood add to the story? How do these two people differ in personality and function?

- What are the differences in interior furnishings between the households of the Linton family and the Earnshaw family? What complications arise from the differences?

- Several characters are associated with animals. What dimensions of their personalities do these associations illuminate?

- What similarities do you perceive between this novel and the sub-plot of Shakespeare's *King Lear*?

- The world in *Wuthering Heights* is both exclusive and inclusive. What considerations in the novel broaden its scope, despite geographical limitations?

THE GOOD EARTH
BY PEARL S. BUCK

SOURCE

Junior High School English 1 and 2, Grade 9. Burbank Unified School District, California. 1987. 474 pp. **ED 296 373**

BRIEF DESCRIPTION

Students participate in a brainstorming and clustering exercise; following the conventional writing form, they tell significant stories from the childhood or adolescent phases of their life.

OBJECTIVE

Students realize that their lives are divided into phases, and they explore the significance of one of these phases.

PROCEDURES

Assign the reading of Pearl S. Buck's *The Good Earth*.

PRE-WRITING ACTIVITY

1. With your class, brainstorm topics that students suggest as they think about their school. Do not be selective at this time. Include every suggestion that anyone makes so that a wealth of ideas is available for the students to refer to while writing their individual papers.

2. After the brainstorming, you and your class may cluster the ideas by arranging them and mapping them according to perceived connections.

WRITING SITUATION

- *The Good Earth* is a chronicle of many phases in Wang Lung's life as he changes from peasant farmer to ricksha driver to rich landlord. Throughout the story, Wang Lung faces several troubled times during which he is mired in problems, yet he always manages to rise above them.

- Think about some of the memorable phases in your life when you faced challenges or problems that you eventually overcame: When you first started school or began at a new school; when you faced death or a great loss; when you tried to fit in or gain acceptance; when you conquered a new sport or other challenge; when you faced a family problem or a friendship problem.

- Choose one phase that extends over several days or weeks to describe to your classmates. The phase will probably include something you learned about yourself and others that was sad, bewildering, frightening, challenging, heart-warming, or illuminating about life and your own human existence.

DIRECTIONS FOR WRITING

- In an autobiographical essay, using ideas from the clustering exercise, tell the story of a significant childhood or adolescent phase from your life.

- Describe the phase in your life using details that appeal to the senses, so that your classmates can identify with your story.

- Show how you met the challenge or resolved the problem. How did you change over the course of events?

- Make sure that your readers will be able to see the special significance this phase held for you.

- What did it mean to you then, and what does it mean to you now?

THE REVISION PROCESS

- Swap essays with a classmate; edit one another's essays.
- Rewrite your own essay in light of your editor's comments.

MIDDLEMARCH
BY GEORGE ELIOT

SOURCE

Cocks, Nancy. "Illuminating the Vision of Ordinary Life: A Tribute to 'Middlemarch,'" *English Journal*, v76 n3 March 1987, pp. 78-81.

BRIEF DESCRIPTION

Students keep a reflections diary, do research, give an oral report, and write a letter.

OBJECTIVE

To enable your students to see that the society in which they live affects the way they live, the jobs they have, and the beliefs they hold.

PROCEDURES

BACKGROUND

The name "George Eliot" is a pseudonym used by Mary Ann Evans, a woman who lived in Victorian England from 1819 to 1880. Victorian society greatly constrained a woman's activities; therefore, Mary Ann Evans wrote using a man's name so that her writing would be published.

REFLECTIONS DIARY

- As you read *Middlemarch*, keep a reflections diary. Record your feelings, quotations that you like, questions that arise, comments that you have on relationships among characters in the story, opinions that you form on life in Victorian society, and your critical judgment of the book.

Oral Report

✦ Do research for an oral report on some aspect of Victorian life. Choose one from the following list of topics. If you have a different idea in mind, check with your teacher to see if it is acceptable.

Shopping for food	Modes of transportation	Being a servant
Art	Music	Theology
Child labor	Class system	Royalty
Economic theory	Job market	Contemporary politics
City life	Country Life	Crystal Palace
Architectural styles	Furniture styles	Clothing Styles
Victorian reform movements	Technological and scientific development	

✦ Select one of the following writing assignments:

1. Imagine that you have children. Write a letter to them revealing your *Middlemarch*-inspired hopes for their future.

2. Write a letter to George Eliot. Tell her what feelings and thoughts *Middlemarch* inspired in you, and how reading the book has affected your life.

3. Write a letter to one of the characters in *Middlemarch*. Think of this character as a friend, and give advice on some aspect of his/her life.

Comments

Middlemarch traces a web of relationships in a cross-section of English society. Its plot is furthered by the idiosyncracies of the class system and its characters' struggle with the big issues of their day: faith, duty, technology, social reform, artistic vision, self-fulfillment. For *Middlemarch's* major characters, however, these big issues and even bigger questions (Who am I? What is the purpose of life? What is the truth about human nature?) arise specifically in the struggle to choose an appropriate vocation and to do it justice.

SUMMER OF MY GERMAN SOLDIER
BY BETTE GREEN

SOURCE

"Course Outlines for English—Junior High School, Grades 7 and 8." Burbank Unified School District, California. September 1987. 463 pp.
ED 296 372

BRIEF DESCRIPTION

Encourages students to explore their feelings and the requirements of friendship as they complete cluster assignments and express their ideas in a written paper.

OBJECTIVE

To develop writing skills using brainstorming and clustering; to hone editing skills.

PROCEDURES

Select one of the following topics to introduce the literature:

1. Discussion of World War II, the Holocaust, and concentration camps
2. Discussion of German POW camps in the United States
3. Discussion of teenagers' feelings of being alienated from their parents
4. Discussion of religious and racial discrimination and stereotyping
5. Time-line of events for World War II
6. Interview of an older member of student's family who remembers World War II (students report findings to class)

Assign the reading of *Summer of My German Soldier* with the following instructions and the editing/proofreading sheet.

+ In *Summer of My German Soldier,* Patty shows that she is a very good friend to Anton. There are many qualities that make a good friend. Our choice of friends may be very important to our lives; therefore, knowing what qualities are important to us is vital to our personal development.

- Write your definition of friendship.
- Brainstorm ways in which Patty was a good friend to Anton.
- Think of someone who has been a good friend to you. List the ways in which that person has been a good friend to you.
- Brainstorm qualities that you think a person must have in order to be a good friend.
- Cluster and think about those qualities that you believe are important in a friend. Write a report in which you explain these qualities. Use your idea clusters to help develop your point of view. Support your selections with details, facts, and examples taken from Bette Green's story.
- Complete the attached editing/proofreading worksheet as you revise and rewrite your essay.

Alternative suggestion: Have your students work in pairs. Each student completes an editing/proofreading sheet for the other student's essay.

Editing/Proofreading Worksheet

Author's Name:_____ Essay's Title: _____

1. I have considered the organization of this essay. The following adjustment in organization might make the essay better: _____
   _____
   _____

2. I have pondered the ideas in this essay. The following ideas are unclear to me:_____
   _____
   _____

3. I have weighed the language of this essay. The following words/phrases seem to require revision:_____
   _____
   _____

4. The essay ____is ____ is not neat and legible.

5. The essay includes incorrect form on the following items:
   _____ heading _____ title _____margins _____ paragraphing/ indentation

6. The following corrections need to be made in the form of this essay:
   _____
   _____
   _____

Novels

7. I have checked each word for correct spelling. The author needs to check the spelling of the following words:

   _____
   _____
   _____

8. I have checked the paper for correct use of capital letters. The author needs to correct the use of capitals on the following words:

   _____
   _____
   _____

9. I have checked each sentence for subject/verb agreement. The following sentence(s) has (have) an error in agreement:

   _____
   _____
   _____

10. The sentence that I liked best:

    _____
    _____
    _____

11. The sentence that needs the most help:

    _____
    _____
    _____

    _____
    Editor's Signature

The Friends
by Rosa Guy

Source

Lesson Plans for Teaching Young Adult Literature, North Carolina State Department of Public Instruction, Raleigh. 1988. 108 pp. **ED 319 063**

Brief Description

Students participate in role-play, write a soap-opera script, construct a collage, write an ending to the novel, complete writing exercises, and answer study-guide questions.

Objective

To alert students to the novel's major conflict, to help students analyze their personal involvement with friends in light of the characters' relationships in the novel.

Procedures

Assign the reading of Rosa Guy's *The Friends* to your students.

Activity One

Before reading *The Friends*, introduce the text by having your students develop a list of reasons for newcomers being either accepted or rejected.

Enlist volunteers to participate in role-play. Outline a situation in which a new student has enrolled in your class. Assign to some of the students the role of accepting the newcomer. Assign to other students the role of rejecting this outsider. Remind students to make the situation as real as possible by including verbal and non-verbal responses that will affect the new student. Now read the first chapter of the novel aloud to the class, and compare the events of chapter one to the previous role-play situation. Ask students to discuss the possible emotional problems that could occur when a newcomer is rejected without a chance for acceptance.

ACTIVITY TWO

After completing *The Friends*, discuss the most dramatic aspects of the novel. Extract several passages from the novel that present a dramatic exchange of feelings. Discuss these passages and explain the illumination apparent in each. Ask your students to discuss how they were personally affected by these revelations.

Following the discussion of the dramatic aspects of the novel, divide the class into small groups. Assign to each group one of the following activities:

1. Choose a part of the novel about which to write a three- or four-scene soap-opera script. The soap opera must be given a fictional title that expresses the conflict. All members in the group are expected to act out parts.

2. Construct a collage that displays some of the emotional exchanges between characters. Each situation represented is to be accompanied by a dramatic oral reading, read as vividly as possible.

3. Write an ending for the novel. Finalize Phyllisia's relationship with Edith, Ruby, Marian, Calvin, José, her classmates, and Ramona's spirit.

4. Identify the "true friend" in the novel; defend your choice with specific evidence from the novel.

5. Gather and/or write poems, songs, and sayings that express the qualities of friendship. Discuss the association of each to the novel.

Allow students to brainstorm ideas about their assignments. Monitor group discussions, and ask your students to turn in a list of possible ideas.

ACTIVITY THREE

After reading chapters 1-3, discuss the following questions with your class. Give all students a copy of the list of questions so that their minds may range over the ideas.

Questions to be asked about THE FRIENDS

1. What point of view is taken?
2. Who is the narrator?
3. Describe Edith Jackson as seen through the eyes of the narrator.
4. How does Edith react to the narrator's snub?
5. How does Phyllisia feel about her new school and classmates?
6. Why is she being ridiculed by her classmates?
7. Among her classmates, which one appears to hate Phyllisia the most?
8. How does Phyllisia feel about her father, Calvin?
9. Why does Phyllisia try to hide her intelligence?
10. What does Phyllisia observe about her teacher, Miss Lass?
11. Why does she need courage to leave the safety of the school building?
12. How does she manage to escape the crowd?
13. Describe Phyllisia's appearance as she walks home.
14. Describe Ramona's attitude towards Phyllisia's predicament.
15. Describe Calvin's attitude towards fighting.
16. Describe the two men who come with Calvin to the apartment.
17. In what ways does Calvin treat his two daughters differently?
18. In spite of Edith's attention, whom does Phyllisia desire to have as a friend?
19. What parallel between Rosa Guy and Phyllisia is shown in the first three chapters of the novel?
20. What motivates the conflict in the novel?
21. Based on the first chapters of the novel, what is the style of writing?

Novels

A Wrinkle in Time
by Madeline L'Engle

Source

"Course Outlines for English—Junior High School, Grades 7 and 8." Burbank Unified School District, California. September 1987. 463 pp.
ED 296 372

Brief Description

Students gain writing experience through journal writing, fiction writing, and comprehension exercises.

Objective

To help students improve their writing and thinking skills.

Procedures

Before reading *A Wrinkle in Time*, ask your students to begin a journal. Ask them to complete their journal entries each day after listening to you read one of the following entries a day for three days.

Day One

Your older brother has disappeared. He was working on a project about time machines for the school's science fair. Your family is terribly upset, for you are a close-knit, happy family. The rumor at school, however, is that he has run away from home. You know this can't be true. Write about how you feel about this situation.

Day Two

You decide to talk to the science teacher because she knew your brother well. You go to her room after school, but she's busy helping another student with his science project. While you wait, you wander over to your brother's project, a contraption built from a piano shipping crate. You step inside it, feeling sad. Despite the tears, you notice a green button has been added since you helped him lug the crate to school. Absentmindedly you push it, thinking about your brother. You look to see if the teacher is still busy. You are shocked that you are neither in the science room nor in even another time. You are on another planet! Look around. Describe this planet and its inhabitants. Use all five of your senses to perceive your new surroundings.

DAY THREE

You are still exploring the new planet. You find your brother. You have a happy reunion. He tells you that neither of you can return to earth unless you are rescued. You ask about the inhabitants, their laws and customs. You also ask the planet's name. What does your brother tell you? After you hear about the planet and its inhabitants, what are your thoughts and feelings?

For extra credit, some students might enjoy completing the story.

Have your students choose one of the following writing projects:

✦ Discuss your opinions of space exploration.

✦ Focusing on the battle between good and evil, devise, name, and organize the traits of an imaginary "good guy" and a "bad guy." Each may have a supernatural power.

✦ Pick a partner and choose one "good guy" and one "bad guy." Write a dialogue between the two. Read your dialogue to the class.
[**Note**: "guy" can refer to either male or female in contemporary American slang.]

Ask students to read *A Wrinkle in Time*.

✦ The philosophy of Camazotz was that all were happy because all were alike. Some teenagers believe this, too; they want to be like their peers. Think about whether you believe in being like your peers or in being unique.

✦ Write a report discussing whether a student can be happier by being like his or her peers or by being unique. State your position clearly. Support your choice with facts, reasons, and examples.

Some of the following questions may be used during a discussion period:

1. State the reasons for Meg's disliking herself.

2. Describe Charles Wallace, and state why people thought he was "dumb."

3. Explain a *tesseract*.

4. Give examples of objects, images, and sensations that Meg experienced with the tesseract.

5. Why did Mrs. Who, Mrs. Whatsit, and Mrs. Which have trouble speaking?

6. Discuss what IT represented.

7. Why did Mr. Murray almost submit to IT?

8. Meg was terribly disappointed to find that her father did not know or do all things. Explain the lesson she learned when she realized the truth.

A Wizard of Earthsea
by Ursula Le Guin

Source

Fox, Geoff. "Notes on 'Teaching' *A Wizard of Earthsea*," *Children's Literature in Education* v11 1973, pp. 58-67.

Brief Description

Students write a spell, concoct an alphabet, fashion a game, and draw pictures.

Objective

To increase comprehension skills by using imaginative processes.

Procedures

Cast-a-Spell

+ Using the Hardad language, write a spell to help Pechvarry's dying child.

+ You may use place names of Earthsea.

+ Write your spell using the runic alphabet, or invent your own alphabet. Be sure to hand in the English translation with the runic version or with your invented alphabet version.

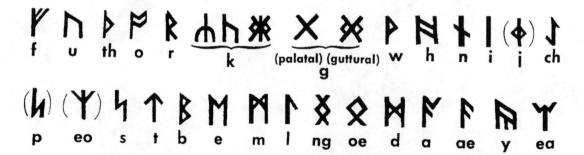

+ The runic alphabet was used by northern Europeans before it was replaced by the Latin alphabet. The runic alphabet is called "Futhork." Why?

Make-a-Game

- Make up a game using the sequence of events in the book.
- It may be played using a gameboard, cards, dice, computer, or it may be an action game.
- For example, you might devise a board game called "The Wizard Game." The gameboard is a map of Gont. The board is divided into a series of squares. The players roll a pair of dice to determine the number of squares on which to move their game pieces. In every third square is a set of instructions that the players are to follow if they land on that square. For example:

  Duny learns goat-spell from Aunt: Advance 4 spaces.

  Duny keeps mist: Throw a 6 before moving on.

  Ged picking herbs: Miss two turns.

  The game is finished when a player reaches Ged's staff.

Draw-a-Drawing

- Select and draw one of the following objects using the book's descriptions as your inspiration:

  The ship *Shadow*

  The Dragon of Pendor

  The Shadow

A Wizard of Earthsea
by Ursula Le Guin

Source

Rollin, Lucy W. "Exploring Earthsea: A Sixth Grade Literature Project," *Children's Literature in Education* v16 n4 Winter 1985, pp. 195-202.

Brief Discussion

In discussing the setting for Earthsea, students are made aware of the differences between realistic books of fiction and fantasy books; they draw pictures of its settings; they discuss its symbols and themes.

Objective

To examine a relatively complex book, and discover meaning in the setting, symbols, and themes.

Procedures

On the chalkboard, write a list of realistic books of fiction that your students may have read.

The Yearling

Johnny Tremain

Harriet the Spy

Julie of the Wolves

From the Mixed-Up Files of Mrs. Basil E. Frankweiler

With your students, discuss time and place in each book, showing them that most of the books take place in the present time and in real places that they can locate on a map.

Read excerpts from fantasy books that mention things from the real world, but in which the time and place are vague.

The Borrowers

Alice in Wonderland

Mrs. Piggle Wiggle

Explain to your students that these books are fantasies, and yet they are still connected to reality.

- What are the time and place of Earthsea?
- Do the time and place of Earthsea really exist?
- Can you locate Earthsea on a map?
- Can you find the time period of Earthsea on an ordinary calendar?

Divide the class into groups. To each group give posterboard and markers. Ask each group to draw pictures of what is real and what is not real in Earthsea. Assign one of the following categories to each group:

Animals: dragon, otak, hawk

People: wizards, witches, sailors, farmers

Plants: strawflowers, fourfoil, white hallows

Islands: an archipelago made up of reaches

The students may use encyclopedias to get ideas. To draw the islands, they may enlarge the map found in their copy of the book. It might be fun to assign a project in which the students are to make a list of herbs and plants mentioned in Earthsea. Then they can do research to see if they are real plants.

SYMBOLS

Show your students a single rose. Discuss with them what the rose might symbolize and why.

- Name some other symbols

    the "Stars and Stripes" (U.S. flag)

    the "Stars and Bars" (Confederate flag)

    Cross

    Star of David

    Swastika

- Name some of the symbols found in Earthsea:

    Shadow

    Ged's staff

    Otak

    Sea

- What do these symbols represent?

THEME

- State some of the themes in *Earthsea*.

    "Death comes to everyone and must be accepted."

    "Caring for humans and other animals is important."

    "Having power is not always good."

- Is there a relationship between the symbols and the themes?

COMMENT

A Wizard of Earthsea is a teachable book, accessible on many levels to middle- and high-schoolers, with many possibilities for enjoyment and for the development of critical skills that help readers enjoy other literature as well.

Novel

Halfway Down Paddy Lane
by Jean Marzollo

Source

Milton, John Whitney. "Teaching the Elements of Fiction Using an Adolescent Novel: Halfway Down Paddy Lane." In Matthews, Dorothy, ed. *On Contemporary Literature: Critiques, Reviews and Recommendations.* Illinois Association of Teachers of English, Urbana, Illinois. 1985. 66 pp. **ED 252 860**

Brief Description

Students complete assignments as they deal with the title, opening, and theme of the novel.

Objective

To discover why one chooses a particular novel; to read actively; to find the theme of a novel.

Procedures

Opening

Do the following exercise before your students read the novel.

Read aloud the following opening passage of the novel.

> *Kate didn't turn or open her eyes. It was as if only her mind had awakened. Something's changed, she thought. Something's wrong.*

Now prompt your students to use their imaginations to predict what happens next:

+ What do you know about the story so far?
+ Write what you think will happen in the next paragraph.

Discuss your students' responses and talk about what it means for an author to set up a story "that's going somewhere."

THEME

- As you read the novel, write down a tentative statement of theme. As you continue to read, revise your statement as necessary to include important details.

  The major theme of the book is an examination of the workings of time. A development of this theme is a comparison of details about living in two different centuries.

- After you have read the book, make a list of similarities and differences between the two centuries involved in the novel.

- List the adjustments that Kate made as she tried to cope in her new time period.

TITLE: CAN YOU TELL A BOOK BY ITS COVER?

The following exercises are to be completed while your students are reading the novel or shortly after.

- Consider the following questions about the novel's title, *Halfway Down Paddy Lane*, as you read the book:

  1. Does *Halfway Down Paddy Lane* refer to rice paddies?

  2. Is "halfway" significant in contrast to "all the way?"

  3. Does "lane" suggest a story that takes place at the edge of a small town?

- Complete the following comparative-analysis exercise. Beside the title of each book, write what you think the title means and why. Also, indicate whether the title of the book sparks your interest to read the book.

  The Shelter Trap

  The Sports Medicine Book

  One Flew over the Cuckoo's Nest

  The Naked and the Dead

  Gone with the Wind

  The Glass Menagerie

  Dinner at the Homesick Restaurant

  The Chocolate War

  The Name of the Rose

  Slaughterhouse-Five

- If you were the author and had written the novel about Kate, name three titles that you might have given the novel.
- Why do you think Jean Marzollo named the novel *Halfway Down Paddy Lane*?

COMMENTS

Halfway Down Paddy Lane is a young-adult novel strong enough to bear the kind of close scrutiny that sophisticated readers bring to serious literature. Not only is it pedagogically valuable but also it is a pleasure to read. Secondary students can understand it easily as a story; for this reason teachers need not explain the plot and may instead concentrate on helping students learn how to analyze fiction. Readers will enjoy the story for its artistry and its insight into the human condition.

Halfway Down Paddy Lane
by Jean Marzollo

Source

Milton, John Whitney. "Teaching the Elements of Fiction Using an Adolescent Novel: Halfway Down Paddy Lane." In Matthews, Dorothy, ed. *On Contemporary Literature: Critiques, Reviews and Recommendations.* Illinois Association of Teachers of English, Urbana, Illinois. 1985. 66 pp. **ED 252 860**

Brief Description

Students answer a series of questions as they read Jean Marzollo's novel, *Halfway Down Paddy Lane.*

Objective

To stimulate a reader to develop from being merely a plot reader to being an evaluator of the aesthetics and thought of a novel.

Procedures

- Answer the following questions as you read Jean Marzollo's novel, *Halfway Down Paddy Lane.*

    1. Why might Marzollo have picked fifteen and eighteen for the ages of Kate and Patrick, since they are considering marriage?

    2. Why might Kate's father, Calambra, and the older Kate's father, O'Hara, be mentioned briefly but not be present in the novel?

    3. Why would Marzollo give only vague and tentative explanations about the mechanism by which Kate traveled through time?

    4. In which month did Kate's adventures begin? Why is it important for Marzollo to specify the month?

    5. The limited omniscient point of view does not allow readers to get inside the thoughts of any character except Kate. Why might Marzollo have elected to deny herself access to Patrick's thoughts?

6. Why might Kate Calambra's mother not have become more suspicious when her daughter was replaced by Kate O'Hara?

7. At the end of the book, why did Kate not want to talk over her experiences with her real mother?

8. Marzollo's plot builds and builds, continually rising towards a moment of highest emotional and thematic significance. Are the emotional and the thematic climaxes the same?

9. Dramatic irony is the double view of a situation in which the audience knows something significant that a character does not. Dramatic irony is thus like a private joke between the writer and the audience. How is the last page an example of dramatic irony? What is its effect?

10. Imagery has the power to convey concisely, indirectly, and cogently a lot of thought, emotion, and imagination. Comment on both the literary and the emotional impact of each of the following images:

    a. Mother O'Hara was described to Nora as "madder than a tricked leprechaun."

    b. After the church was destroyed, Kate and Patrick "hugged so tight, it was as if the fire they felt in their burned skins welded them together."

    c. In the mill, "Kate moved like a machine."

    d. Fleeing Patrick and Nora on her way to Lowell, Kate felt her "heart pressed into a small cold metal box."

Comments

The appeal of the plot of *Halfway Down Paddy Lane* owes much to its skillful exploitation of conflict. Unsophisticated students find it useful to recognize four general types of conflict as the basis on which a story is built: person against society, person against person, person against nature, and person against self. It is a measure both of Marzollo's skill as a writer and of the depth of her heroine's dilemma that Kate could be said to have some degree of conflict with everything about her breathtaking new life.

Anne of Green Gables

by L. M. Montgomery

Source

Lesson Plans for Teaching Young Adult Literature. North Carolina State Department of Public Instruction, Raleigh. 1988. 108 pp. **ED 319 063**

Brief Description

Based on chapters 15-17 of *Anne of Green Gables*, students prioritize values, connect values with decisions, and participate in a debate. Students learn that making decisions is based on values; they generate ideas and supporting details; they exchange ideas that generate contrasting values.

Objective

To make students comfortable when expressing ideas in small groups; to stimulate students to "work" with their value structures.

Procedures

Assign the reading of chapters 15-17 of L. M. Montgomery's *Anne of Green Gables*.

Focus/Review

The chief conflict in chapter 14 centers on Marilla's reaction when she thought that Anne had lied about stealing a brooch. Her decision to punish Anne by making her stay in her room until she confessed is a direct result of the high value that Marilla places on honesty. Anne's confession is a direct result of the great importance that she places on friendship and ice cream. Other decisions of characters emphasize their own values. The values we prize direct the ways we live our lives.

Teacher Input and Guided Practice

Characters in stories, like people in real life, make decisions based on what they believe to be valuable. Sometimes, conflict arises within oneself because individuals hold conflicting values simultaneously. For example, a student may value honesty and a high test score at the same time: Internal conflict arises in making the decision whether or not to cheat on a test. Moreover, one person's set of values may conflict with another person's set of values, for people perceive the relative importance of values differently from each other. The following activity shows the importance of values and, at the same time, the difficulty and relativity involved in rank-ordering them.

1. Divide your class into groups of five. Give each student a copy of the values-ranking activity (see next page). Read the instructions, and answer any questions. Allow five minutes for individual work, and fifteen minutes for group discussions.

2. Divide your class into two groups. Pose a debatable topic such as "Anne has excessive pride." Let one group affirm the idea that she does have, and the other group, that she does not have, "excessive pride." Each student is to propose specific details in defense of his or her argument.

Closure

Whether a character (or a real-life person) is conscious of it or not, one's life is molded by one's strong beliefs in specific principles. The importance that one places on certain values determines a person's path in life.

Rank-order Your Values

- Working alone, rank each of the values listed below in the order in which you believe they are important. Rank from highest to lowest in importance until all values are ranked.

- Discuss the rank order of values of each member of your group. State your position as logically as you can. Think of reasons for your decisions. Listen carefully to the logic and reasons that other members of your group present for their order of values.

- Your group is to reach consensus on a common ranking.

____ pleasure	____ obedience	____ wisdom
____ family stability	____ love	____ happiness
____ self-respect	____ honesty	____ loyalty
____ work	____ pride	____ creativity
____ fairness	____ beauty	____ morally acceptable behavior

After fifteen minutes, the entire class may discuss the following:

- What value was the easiest to rank? Why?

- What value was the most difficult to rank? Why?

- The choices of characters in chapters 15-17 are based on similar values. Give the value behind the following decisions made by the characters:

    1. Anne and Diana decide to go to school by Lover's Lane and Willowmere.

    2. Anne does not like the teacher because he helped Prissy Andrews.

    3. Marilla is concerned that Anne was "a good girl" at school.

    4. Diana says that being smart is better than being good-looking.

    5. Anne ignores Gilbert Blythe after he called her "Carrots."

    6. Anne feels insulted when she had to sit with Gilbert.

    7. Anne refuses to go back to school for a while.

    8. Think of some decision that a character makes in Chapter 16. What options were available? What values influenced the decision? Would another character have acted the same way?

    9. In chapter 17, Anne returns to school and is very studious. Why do you think she returned to school?

ANNE OF GREEN GABLES

BY L. M. MONTGOMERY

SOURCE

Lesson Plans for Teaching Young Adult Literature. North Carolina State Department of Public Instruction, Raleigh. 1988. 108 pp. **ED 319 063**

BRIEF DESCRIPTION

Based on chapters 36-38 of *Anne of Green Gables*, students role-play attitudes, participate in group discussion, search for changes in characters, and work independently on a project.

OBJECTIVE

To show students that characters change in some ways, but not in others; to distinguish between static and dynamic characters.

PROCEDURES

Assign the reading of chapters 36-38 in L. M. Montgomery's *Anne of Green Gables.*

TEACHER INPUT

Chapter 35 deals with Anne's life at Queen's. Anne had been an excellent student while living at home, and she continued to excel in the new school. Also, the competition between Anne and Gilbert continued, even though neither would admit openly the importance of the other's effort. Although many other things in the lives of the characters remained constant, there were changes in some beliefs and attitudes.

Basically characters fall into two type: static and dynamic, non-changing and changing.

A static character remains the same throughout the story. Sometimes, an author's purpose is to show that a character cannot change. For example, a character may not change the desire for something and, as a result, will die fighting even for a lost cause.

A dynamic character changes. This character may reform, may come to see another person in a different way, may grow in understanding, may mature, or may learn responsibility instead of waiting for other people to do the work.

To illustrate these two terms, have students role-play, and then discuss, the roles played. You may use scenes from the novel or general ideas for role-playing. In either case, the details are to be improvised: no script. The following ideas work as starters:

1. An angry mother waiting late at night for a son or daughter to return home from a party

2. A high-school student trying to calm an upset parent over low grades on a report card

3. A police officer giving a driver a ticket for speeding

4. Matthew's attitude toward Anne the first time he met her and took her home

5. Anne's attitude toward Gilbert when he made fun of her hair

6. Anne's attitude toward Diana as expressed in the scene with Diana after Anne returned home from school

7. Anne's attitude toward Marilla when she found out that Marilla was thinking about selling the farm

Discuss the following questions regarding the characters in your role play:

✦ Is there a change in the importance of the characters as they themselves change?

✦ Do the characters' attitudes change towards a friend, a disease, or a girl?

✦ Do the characters begin to resent, regret, or accept a person or thing?

GUIDED PRACTICE

First, analyze the last three chapters of the novel for change of character. Then allow students to discuss other changes. The following may be used to begin the discussion:

1. At the commencement, Matthew and Marilla "were there, with eyes and ears for only one student on the platform—a tall girl...."

2. "Well now, I'd rather have you than a dozen boys, Anne...it wasn't a boy that took the Avery scholarship...it was a girl—my girl...." (said Matthew)

3. "It was the last night before sorrow touched her life, and no life is ever quite the same again when once that cold, sanctifying touch has been laid upon it."

4. Marilla is strict and, sometimes, harsh with Anne.

5. Marilla is not able to express her feelings openly.

6. Anne loves Matthew and Marilla.

7. Anne worries about personal beauty.

8. Anne desires a formal education.

9. Anne covets the Avery scholarship.

10. Gilbert's feelings towards Anne

11. Anne's feelings towards Gilbert

INDEPENDENT PROJECTS

Invite your students to undertake one of the following projects. Give them more than one day to complete the assignment.

1. Draw a map locating key places in the novel.

2. Design a newspaper based on important events in the novel. Include news items, human-interest stories, letters to the editor, editorials, feature columns and departments, advertisements, deaths, etc.

3. Be a character in the book, and review some of the most interesting experiences that happened to that character. Wear a costume suited for the character, if you like, when you give the oral presentation.

4. Revise a scene from the novel into a play. Several of you perform the scene before the class.

5. Give a television show in which someone interviews two or three characters from the novel.

6. Write a biography of one of the characters. Be sure to include such points as background, how others feel about the character, and the characters' values, goals and ambitions, and his or her physical appearance.

7. Based on character development in the novel, write a letter from one character to another.

8. Select several meaningful quotations from the novel and explain them.

9. Select at least five unusual words and explain them in context.

10. Prepare a poster of several symbols and key places in the novel. Be able to explain your poster to the class.

Closure

The individuality of a character is developed through unique responses to situations and people. What happens is not nearly so important as the person to whom something happens. Someone with less sensitivity to nature and to people than Anne had, would not have loved the life offered at Green Gables so thoroughly as she did.

Sula / Song of Solomon / Tar Baby

by Toni Morrison

Source

Nichols, Julie J. "Patterns in Toni Morrison's Novels," *English Journal*, v72 n1 January 1983, pp. 46-48.

Brief Description

Students answer assigned questions as a group, write individual essays, complete a research project, and complete a writing project.

Objective

To discuss the individual and cumulative effects of novels dealing with complex social issues; to discuss the literary devices of structure and pattern.

Procedures

Divide the class into three groups. Ask each group to choose one student who will be responsible for organizing the presentation of the group's ideas to the rest of the class. Assign one of the following three books by Toni Morrison to each group: *Song of Solomon* or *Sula* or *Tar Baby*

- Answer the following questions for the novel that you are reading:

    1. What happens in the story? Summarize the plot.

    2. Choose one or two words used repeatedly throughout the novel. Tell how these words change or grow in meaning or in importance from the beginning of the story until the end.

    3. How do you feel at the end? Is everything resolved? What kind of epilogue would you write?

    4. What does the novel say about Black people? Do you think the view of Black people in the story is accurate? Why do you think so, or why not?

Do some research on the history and influence of local traditions, and write an essay on one of the following themes:

> The Rose Parade on New Year's Day in Pasadena, California
>
> Eating turkey on Thanksgiving Day
>
> Santa Claus leaving gifts at Christmas
>
> Throwing rice/bird seed after weddings
>
> Trick-or-treating at Halloween
>
> Exchanging Valentine's cards on Valentine's Day
>
> Mother's Day/Father's Day
>
> Tying cans on the back bumper of a car at weddings

Assign one of the following writing projects to each group:

1. **Sula**

    a. Do you have a friend who is like you in many ways but also different? Write an essay in which you envision your two futures.

    b. Suppose you left your town for ten years and then returned. Write an article for a newspaper or magazine describing the changes you see. Are they good or bad changes? What things have remained the same? Is this good or bad?

    c. Write a series of letters between two friends who have shared their childhood and high-school years but have not seen each other for ten years.

2. **Song of Solomon**

    a. Tell about the effect of your immediate family on you. Would you like to know more about your ancestors? What kind of effect do you suppose they have on your life?

    b. "What's in a name?" Tell about someone, real or imagined, whose name is unusual or was given for what you consider was a peculiar reason. Tell about the effect of that person's name on his or her life.

    c. Make up a story about the origin of a nursery rhyme or game song. Do some research in the library to find out the other astonishing historical meanings of children's rhymes and games and songs, such as "Ring around the Rosie" and "London Bridge."

3. **Tar Baby**

    a. What is a tar baby? Why is that the title of the book? Do you think it is appropriate? What other name would you give it?

    b. Why do you think Michael is in the book? If you were Ondine, would you have kept his secret—or would you have kept his mother's secret?

    c. Write Valerian's journal for the period covered in the novel, and then write Sydney's.

COMMENTS

Toni Morrison's novels will heighten your awareness of the Black consciousness informed by the rich interweaving of Biblical and other images. The patterns in all three novels, with their individual and cumulative effects, are impressive. They are good books to discuss with advanced classes ready to handle complex social issues (Black versus White, man versus woman) and literary devices such as structure and pattern.

THE YEARLING

MARJORIE RAWLINGS

SOURCE

"Junior High School English 1 and 2, Grade 9." Burbank Unified School District, California. 1987. 474 pp. **ED 296 373**

BRIEF DESCRIPTION

Students delve into the responsibility of pet ownership by answering probing questions, developing their vocabularies, and writing essays.

OBJECTIVE

Students expand their comprehension abilities, enlarge their vocabularies, and strengthen their writing skills.

PROCEDURES

INTRODUCTION

Introduce the work by engaging in the following class conversation:

- How many of you have ever had family pets?
- Have you ever had your own pet?
- Has your pet ever gotten into mischief?
- What attributes in a person does having a pet develop? (Care, love, responsibility)
- What are some of the difficulties that you have encountered when you had a pet? (The chores of feeding and watering, growing up, traveling and moving, accidents and mischief, aging and death)
- Why would having a pet, particularly for an only child, have been more special in pioneer times?
- What is dialect?

Assign the reading of Marjorie Rawlings's *The Yearling*.

Novels

ONGOING COMPREHENSION ACTIVITIES

- Discuss the difference between the relationship of Jody to Penny and Jody to his mother. Does this typify kids' relationships with their parents?

- How is Jody like you? How is he different?

- What are values? How does Penny teach Jody values? How have your values been taught to you?

- What is the literary purpose of Fodder-wing in the story? Grandma Hutto?

- To which character are you most drawn? Why?

- Make your own map of the area, including Baxter's Island, the Forresters, Grandma Hutto, Volusia, and the river areas.

WRITING SITUATION

- At some point in your life, an experience with an animal (or a possession) has helped you learn a lesson about life. Reflect on this lesson and how it was learned.

DIRECTIONS FOR WRITING

- Write a two-paragraph essay recreating for your reader the experience in which your animal (or possession) helped you learn a lesson. Interpret and/or reflect on this lesson, describing the details of the incident and the feelings you experienced. (This can be written in the third person, i.e., you, the author, are a witness describing the events rather than a doer doing them.) Make sure that the "lesson" you learned is clearly presented to your reader.

Vocabulary Development

◆ Choose one of the following words that best defines the word(s) in bold.

1. If only Penny could have been **trussed up**, he might have prevented the fawn from getting the corn.
   a. encouraged
   b. supported
   c. abominated
   d. pummeled
   e. none of these

2. The **concern** Ma had for their year's supply of food had made her somewhat disagreeable.
   a. sorties
   b. intricacies
   c. capers
   d. solicitude
   e. none of these

3. The sight of Eulalie Boyle's freckled face **angered** Jody.
   a. lamented
   b. abominated
   c. humiliated
   d. infuriated
   e. none of these

4. Penny's old girl friend, Nellie, **amiably** passed on the word to Ma Baxter that Jody and Penny were okay.
   a. secretly
   b. pleasantly
   c. calmly
   d. uncertainly
   e. none of these

5. Jody's hard work of replanting the corn and building the fence had temporarily **appeased** Ma and Penny's frustration.
   a. subsided
   b. filled
   c. satisfied
   d. reduced
   e. none of these

6. Jody lay beside Flag at the sink hole, **devastated** at the prospect of what was to be the consequences of Flag's mischief.
   a. desolate
   b. ludicrous
   c. inaudible
   d. tacit
   e. none of these

7. Jody **complacently** hitched old Caesar to the wagon for hauling the rails to the corn field.
   a. pleasantly
   b. disinterestedly
   c. uncertainly
   d. self-satisified
   e. none of these

8. Jody spotted the **pendulous** Spanish moss that had reminded Fodder-wing of the helmeted Spaniard on horseback.
   a. unyielding
   b. quiet
   c. loosely hanging
   d. plentiful
   e. none of these

9. The Forresters had **surreptitiously** spirited off the Baxter hogs and penned them.
   a. secretly
   b. doubtfully
   c. lazily
   d. forlornly
   e. none of these

10. The **turgid** sluiceway was impassable and Penny and Jody turned back.
    a. filthy
    b. dreadful
    c. swollen
    d. bold
    e. none of these

THE LATE GREAT ME

BY SANDRA SCOPPETTONE

SOURCE

Lesson Plans for Teaching Young Adult Literature. North Carolina State Department of Public Instruction, Raleigh. 1988. 108 pp. **ED 319 063**

BRIEF DESCRIPTION

Students write a letter to "Dear Abby," write character sketches, and compare/contrast life in two time frames (the 1950s and the 1970s).

OBJECTIVE

Students learn the need to seek help in situations too big to handle alone; to recognize personality traits of characters; and to compare/contrast two time periods.

PROCEDURES

Assign the reading of Sandra Scoppettone's *The Late Great Me.*

ACTIVITY ONE

- In *The Late Great Me,* Geri's friend B.J. tries to convince Geri that drinking will be a destructive force in her life if she doesn't stop. Geri refuses to heed B.J.'s advice. B.J. gives up on Geri instead of seeking help for her as a friend might. In this writing activity, we want to give B.J. a chance to seek help for her friend who truly needs help, even though Geri will not admit it.

- There will possibly come a time in your life when you have a friend who is in trouble and needs your help. Being young and perhaps inexperienced in the problem area, you might not have an answer that your friend can use. Before admitting defeat, you need to seek advice from someone whom you respect and trust and, perhaps from someone who has had some experience in a similar situation. This person may be able to tell you what steps to take to help your friend.

- Assume the role of B.J. Write a "Dear Abby" letter in which you discuss your relationship with Geri, the severity of her drinking problem, and—

thinking back over the novel—offer some insight as to why Geri has this problem. Finally, ask for "Dear Abby's" advice on ways that you can help Geri.

Activity Two

Discuss with your students the definition of "characterization." Stress the importance of characters in literature.

Write the names of the major characters in this book on the chalkboard or overhead projection. Ask your students to center their thoughts on why the characters acted as they did.

Ask for student input regarding characteristics of various characters. Write students' responses under the characters' names.

- Pick any three characters and make a list of personality traits and characteristics for each.

- Write a one-page character sketch for each of these characters.

Activity Three

Geri's mother was obsessed with the past (the 1950s in particular).

You might like to give a brief lecture on the '50s, including politics, entertainment, education, slang expressions, and customs.

- List references made to the 1950s in *The Late Great Me*.

As your students recall the references, write them on the chalkboard. Divide the references into columns labeled "music," "dating customs," "dress," and "female roles."

- Note the differences between the list on the chalkboard and life in the 1970s, according to Geri.

- Write a five-paragraph essay comparing the two different time periods: an introductory paragraph, one paragraph for each of three items taken from the list, and a concluding paragraph.

FRANKENSTEIN

BY MARY SHELLEY

SOURCE

Veidemanis, Gladys V. "*Frankenstein* in the Classroom." *English Journal*, v75 n7 Nov 1986, pp. 61-66.

BRIEF DESCRIPTION

Students select a writing project in which they can stretch their imaginations, write analytically, or do research.

OBJECTIVE

To delve into the world of Dr. Frankenstein and his monster, which is a mine of ideas for writing, speaking, and research.

PROCEDURES

Frankenstein is a story that stirs the imaginative mind to emulation, the curious to research, and the thoughtful to analysis and philosophic speculation. Offer the following topics to your students for writing and research, with the option of choosing what seizes their fancy.

STRETCHING THE IMAGINATION

- Try your hand at writing a ghost or monster story, one with credible characters and intriguing settings. Tape-record your story to be played to the class on a fittingly "dark and dreary" afternoon.

- Write a sequel to the novel—either a continuation of Walton's or of the monster's story. You might follow the monster to the North Pole, to the place of his self-immolation. In the novel, he promises to kill himself, but can we be absolutely sure that he fulfilled his promise? Has Walton "learned his lesson," or has he, instead, aspired too high to turn back?

- Frankenstein chooses not to create a bride for the monster, but Hollywood insisted on speculating about the effect of wife and family on Frankenstein's character; hence films like *Bride of Frankenstein, Son of Frankenstein,* and so forth. Write your own account of the monster united with a mate. Would the two retreat into isolation, as the monster avowed, or, as Frankenstein feared, spawn a hateful and vindictive race to threaten and overwhelm humankind?

ANALYTICAL WRITING

- "Mary's Monster" is far more complex and philosophically interesting than the grotesque monster portrayed in the movies. Contrast the public conception of the monster with the multi-faceted creature portrayed in the novel, not failing to illuminate the monster as an inextricable part of Dr. Frankenstein himself.

- Trace the multiple levels of Dr. Frankenstein's characterization: the family man, the scientist, the Promethean/Faustian figure, the "Ancient Mariner," the fallen angel. What final judgment are we intended to make of this man? What makes him noble in spite of his suffering, failures, and ultimate defeat?

- Analyze Walton's character and functions in the novel, noting analogies to Coleridge's "Wedding Guest" and to Dr. Frankenstein himself. Describe Walton's past history, his reasons for journeying to the North Pole, and the emotional and psychological states of mind that he depicts in his four letters to his sister. Trace his relationship to Dr. Frankenstein from the time he rescues him from the ice floe until his death on the ice-bound ship. What does Walton learn from this extended and most memorable encounter? Has he been "saved" in time by the obsessed scientist, or is he destined to suffer a comparable fate?

RESEARCH TOPICS FOR THE INTELLECTUALLY CURIOUS

- Trace the evolution of the Frankenstein myth as it has been changed and developed from the novel through drama and mass media. Pay particular attention to various film versions of the story, both serious and comic. (See Martin Tropp, *Mary Shelly's Monster*. Boston: Houghton Mifflin, 1976.)

- Select one of Mary Shelley's other novels for reading and study (most recommended, *The Last Man*). Find out what the critics have to say about this book. Explain how this novel compares in themes and style with Frankenstein.

- Investigate current developments in the field of biological and genetic engineering. Present what you consider to be both positive and negative aspects of this research. What moral issues need to be considered as scientists push ahead in this area?

Comments

"'We will each write a ghost story,' said Lord Byron; and his proposition was acceded to." So wrote Mary Shelley, describing the circumstances that motivated the writing of her book. Following a horrifying dream, Mary Shelley, young and gifted (not quite 19 years old), completed her half of the the agreement with her lover, although Lord Byron never wrote his ghost story. The result of Shelley's efforts is a tale that has exerted an hypnotic force on a multitude of readers, for she invented a genuine myth, one that has captured the public fancy and the attention of increasing numbers of literary scholars, not to mention haunting many a private nightmare.

Uncle Tom's Cabin

by Harriet Beecher Stowe

SOURCE

Bennett, Paul W. "A Simulated Street Trial in the Old South." *OAH Magazine of History,* v1 n2 Fall 1985, pp. 23-26.

BRIEF DESCRIPTION

Students participate in role-play intended to simulate a street trial centering on the issue of American slavery in the years before the Civil War. Role players are expected to research and present their positions, act out specific roles, and join in the debate over the question of slavery.

OBJECTIVE

Students strive to gain an accurate understanding of 19th-century American Slavery and to represent conflicting views of slavery.

PROCEDURES

The following role-playing exercise may be used well in conjunction with the reading of Harriet Beecher Stowe's *Uncle Tom's Cabin*. Role players take their parts in the following scenario:

ABOLITIONISM UNDER ATTACK: THE SCENE

Harriet Beecher Stowe, the American abolitionist and author of the popular novel *Uncle Tom's Cabin* (1852), has been apprehended during a secret trip through the southern United States, and she will be publicly questioned by the leading advocates of slavery in the South in the year 1858. The place is Jackson, Mississippi. A street trial has been convened to hear the charges against Stowe, to provide her with an opportunity to present the abolitionist case, and to decide her fate.

THE CHARACTERS

Harriet Beecher Stowe, Defendant—Stowe was not an active abolitionist, and she had reportedly seen slaves only once, during a visit to a Kentucky plantation; nevertheless, her book, *Uncle Tom's Cabin,* presented a searing indictment of the South's "peculiar institution."

Chief Prosecutor

Accusers:

John C. Calhoun—a leading statesman from South Carolina who viewed slavery as "a good—a positive good." His pro-slavery arguments emphasized the harmony of political relations in the South.

Thomas R. Dew—a professor of political economy at William and Mary College in Virginia. Dew was a Southerner who warned that emancipation would bring great disruption to society in the South.

George Fitzhugh—a Virginia writer, lawyer, and social philosopher, regarded as the most noted of the South's pro-slavery intellectuals. To him, slavery was a benevolent, patriarchal system that ensured harmonious relations between social classes.

James Henry Hammond—a wealthy South Carolina lawyer and editor, Hammond was twice elected governor, and he served in Congress in the 1850s. He gained notoriety for his view of Blacks as the virtual "mud sill" of society.

George Frederick Holmes—a distinguished professor of history and literature at the University of Virginia and the foremost critic of *Uncle Tom's Cabin.*

Josiah Nott—a physician and medical scholar from Mobile, Alabama, who applied scientific theories to explain the origin of the races and who contended that the Black race was biologically inferior. In his view, this justified the institution of slavery.

Edmund Ruffin—a native Virginian famous in the South as a scientific agriculturalist, a strident secessionist, and a fluent defender of slavery. In *Political Economy of Slavery* (1853) he set out the argument that slavery conferred many blessings on the Black slave.

Rev. Thornton Stringfellow—a Baptist minister from Culpepper County, Virginia, and one of the most forceful proponents of Biblical scripture in defense of slavery. He found historical and religious justification for slavery in the Hebrew Law and in the Christian New Testament.

Defense Attorneys (one or two people)

Witnesses for the Defense:

Benjamin Lundy—a Quaker and saddle maker from New Jersey and an early leader in the movement to abolish slavery. In 1821, he began to publish a weekly antislavery newspaper in Baltimore, the *Genius of Universal Emancipation.*

William Lloyd Garrison—a radical abolitionist from Massachusetts who rose to prominence as the publisher of *The Liberator*, an antislavery newspaper founded in 1831. Garrison attacked Southern slave owners and Northerners alike who either apologized for slavery or kept silent about it.

Frederick Douglass—a fugitive slave from Maryland and the most famous Black abolitionist of the 1840s and 1850s. A powerful orator, Douglass emerged as an effective campaigner for the American Anti-Slavery Society. At first, he followed the lead of Garrison, but eventually he adopted a more moderate approach and published his own abolitionist paper, the *North Star*. Douglass was active in aiding fugitive slaves to escape via the Underground Railroad.

John Brown—an ardent and erratic Kansas antislavery agitator. In May, Brown avenged an attack on an anti-slavery settlement at Lawrence, Kansas, by launching a bloody retaliatory raid on a group of pro-slavery settlers at Potawatamie Creek, Kansas. Three years later, Brown attempted to stage a slave insurrection at Harper's Ferry, Virginia, but no slaves joined his rebellion, and the attack was quelled by U.S. Marines. Brown's hanging in 1859 made him a martyr of the abolitionist cause.

Abraham Lincoln—a former Whig politician born in a Kentucky log cabin, raised in Indiana, practiced law in Illinois, who first gained national recognition as the Republican candidate for U.S. Senator from Illinois in 1858. Lincoln was not an abolitionist, but he held that slavery was morally wrong and that the institution should not be extended into any of the new territories.

Stephen A. Douglas—Democratic Senator from Illinois and a skillful politician who had helped Henry Clay push through the Compromise of 1850. Douglas vigorously defended the doctrine of "popular sovereignty," and he argued that the residents of a new territory had the right to decide for themselves whether or not to adopt slavery.

The Street Jury (8 to 18 people)

Total number of participants 25 to 35

Preparatory Work

One or two class periods can be set aside for briefing and student preparation.

1. The simulation is introduced and its purposes explained.

2. All students read Harriet Beecher Stowe's *Uncle Tom's Cabin* and any relevant information on slavery and abolitionism that you and they might want to introduce.

3. The roles for the simulation are assigned. All students are to act a part, no matter how small, in the play.

4. Role players research their roles and positions on slavery by using background readings, speeches, articles, and statements.

5. All participants are expected to produce a position paper outlining their views on the slavery issue. The papers are to be submitted for formal evaluation at the end of the exercise.

Sources

Information on the accusers can be found in Eric L. McKitrick, ed., *Slavery Defended: The Views of the Old South* (Englewood Cliffs, N.J.: Prentice-Hall, 1963).

Information on the defenders can be found in Dumas Malone, ed., *Dictionary of American Biography* (New York: Charles Scribner's Sons, 1933, 1961).

For information about Frederick Douglass and William Lloyd Garrison, consult Martin Duberman, ed., *The Antislavery Vanguard* (Princeton: Princeton University Press, 1965).

For information about Abraham Lincoln and Stephen A. Douglas, consult Richard Hofstadter, ed., *Great Issues in American History* (New York: Vintage Books, 1969).

A Summary of the Exercise

The setting and atmosphere are extremely important in generating the proper mood and sense of historical authenticity. Arrange the furniture in your classroom like a courtroom. The Defendant and the Chief Prosecutor might be seated at the front, and the balance of the class divided into three separate delegations: the Accusers, the Defense Witnesses, and the Street Jury. To heighten the air of confrontation, the Defendant might be seated facing both the Accusers and the Street Jury.

Day One: The Charges

1. The Chief Prosecutor calls the court to order and begins by asking the Defendant to stand. The Prosecutor proceeds to read the charges against her. These charges have been developed by the Prosecutor in prior consultation with the Accusers.

2. The Defendant rises to enter a plea and to make a brief appeal for support from the assembled group of Southerners.

3. The Chief Prosecutor calls upon each Accuser in turn to state his or her case against Harriet Beecher Stowe and the abolitionist movement. Each accuser rises and reads his or her indictment, based on actual historical evidence.

4. The Chief Prosecutor asks for further charges from the Street Jury. Members of the audience enter the proceedings, leveling other charges against the Defendant.

5. The street court is recessed to allow time for the Defendant and her witnesses to prepare their case.

Day Two: The Defense

1. The Chief Prosecutor presides. He calls upon the Defense Attorney(s) for a brief introductory statement to the Street Jury.

2. The Defense Attorney(s) then call(s) forward the Witnesses for the Defense, beginning with Benjamin Lundy and continuing in rough chronological sequence through the other witnesses.

3. Each Defense Witness states his or her position and offers a brief defense of Harriet Beecher Stowe and the abolitionist cause.

4. Once the Defense Witnesses have spoken, the Chief Prosecutor opens the court to questions from both the Accusers and the Street Jury. Defense counsel and witnesses are permitted to respond to questions.

5. The Chief Prosecutor announces a recess and asks both the Accusers and the Defense to prepare their final summations.

Day Three: The Final Summations

1. The Chief Prosecutor calls the street court to order and reminds the Jury of its responsibilities.

2. The Defense Attorneys make their final summation to the Street Jury, defending Harriet Beecher Stowe against the charges and accusations.

3. The Chief Prosecutor calls upon John C. Calhoun or another of the Accusers to summarize the case against the Defendant.

4. The Defendant is cross-examined by the Chief Prosecutor and members of the Street Jury.

5. The Chief Prosecutor instructs one of the Jury members to act as chairperson to coordinate the Jury's deliberations. The court is adjourned so the Jury can meet and reach a verdict. (The class may listen to the Jury's deliberation, but only in total silence, as if they were not there.)

DAY FOUR: THE DECISION AND ITS MEANING

1. The Chief Prosecutor calls the street court to order. The Defendant is asked to rise, and the charges are again read to the court.

2. The Jury chairperson reads the verdict and offers an explanation for the Jury's decision.

3. The Chief Prosecutor delivers the sentence. The Defendant is either deported from the South and barred from future entry into the slave States, or released to continue her travels through the States of the South.

4. The court is adjourned.

Reviewing the lessons of the simulation is an essential part of the exercise. The exercise addresses many aspects of the slavery question, among them the following:

1. Culture and identity in the antebellum South
2. *Uncle Tom's Cabin* and its significance
3. The Southern defense of slavery
4. The views of early abolitionists
5. The contending views of Lincoln and Douglas
6. The significance of slavery to the coming of the Civil War

These points might be thoroughly discussed following the conclusion of the simulation, before students are asked to develop their position papers.

EVALUATION

Assessing student performance in simulations like this one is never an easy task. Because the activity emphasizes oral and written communication skills, both of these areas should be evaluated. While much of the oral evaluation is admittedly highly subjective, a checklist evaluation form might be used to show student performance based on a set of criteria. Formally evaluating student performance in the simulation can be a vitally important part of the learning process. If your school has a video camera, one of the best ways to assess individual performances is to videotape the simulation, and then invite your students to engage in self-evaluation and assessment of one another's performances, making use of the checklist of criteria. The position papers should offer a good deal of information about how much the students learned from their participation in the activity.

ROLL OF THUNDER, HEAR MY CRY
BY MILDRED TAYLOR

SOURCE

"Course Outlines for English—Junior High School, Grades 7 and 8." Burbank Unified School District, California. September 1987. 463 pp. ED 296 372

BRIEF DESCRIPTION

Students gain writing experience through brainstorming and clustering, essay writing, and revision.

OBJECTIVE

To help students improve their writing and thinking skills.

PROCEDURE

Assign the reading of *Roll of Thunder, Hear My Cry*.

Have your class brainstorm an imaginary physical description of Mildred Taylor's father. Also brainstorm a personality description of Taylor's father from the "Author's Note" at the beginning of the book. Imagine the ways that Taylor's father influenced her.

Then ask your students to identify the central emotion or strong feelings that Mildred Taylor conveys for her father in her "Author's Note."

Set up the following writing situation for your students:

- The people we know, especially the people we feel strongly about, help shape our personalities. We tend to emulate people we admire, and avoid those characteristics that annoy us in people we dislike. Your classmates and teacher want to know about one of the people who has made an impression on you.

- Select someone you have felt strongly about (admired, feared, hated). Brainstorm silently to develop a physical description of this person, a personality/psychological description, and a description of the influence/effect that the person had on you.

Novels

- Sort the characteristics into logical clusters, and write a two- or three-paragraph biographical essay describing this person. Include detailed physical and psychological descriptions of the person you have chosen to write about. Explain why you felt so strongly about this person and how this person has influenced your life.

Stress the three foci of the biographical sketch.

   a. Physical/psychological description

   b. How the writer feels about the person

   c. How the person influenced the writer

Ask your students to exchange sketches with one another and to check what they have written by using the "Response/Revision Guide." (See next page.)

Ask your students to use the responses they received in the "Response/Revision Guide" as a guide for revising the sketch during the rewrite.

Response/Revision Guide—Biographical Sketch
(Use in responding and revision steps of the writing process)

1. Has the writer used enough sensory details so that you can picture the person sketched in your mind?

2. Has the writer adequately described the type of person whom he or she is sketching?

3. What is your overall impression about the person sketched?

4. How does the writer feel about the person?

5. Why does he or she feel this way?

6. How has the person affected the writer's life or personality?

7. Is the sketch well-organized? If not, what parts could be improved?

8. Are there any parts of the sketch that need more detail or explanation? Explain.

9. Are there any sections that seem awkward or confusing? Explain.

10. Are there any sections that are off-topic? Explain.

11. What did you like best about the sketch?

12. What part of the sketch needs the greatest revision? Why?

Dinner at the Homesick Restaurant

by Anne Tyler

Source

Aronowitz, Beverly Lynne. "R.S.V.P. Another Meal at the Homesick Restaurant: Teaching Theme through Statement," *Exercise Exchange,* v29, n2 Spring 1984, pp. 5-6.

Brief Description

Students select a thematic statement and write an analytical essay.

Objective

Assists students to focus their reading; to see one topic above all the others in a complex novel.

Procedures

Because the novel *Dinner at the Homesick Restaurant* is episodic with a large cast of characters, it presents problems for some readers. Help your students to focus on one meaningful aspect of the text by relating a general statement to the specifics of the novel as they read.

Before they begin reading the novel, give your students a set of declarative statements related to the novel. These statements are meant to stimulate thinking about one character or about one characteristic shared by a few characters. Ask your students to test the generalization against a character or situation as a means of determining the relevancy of the statement and judging how far they may elaborate the relationships among the characters and imagine the cause/effect nexus among the events without offending the inherent logic of the story.

Photocopy the following set of thesis statements, and distribute copies to your students.

Thesis Statements to Define Theme in Anne Tyler's
Dinner at the Homesick Restaurant

1. For no apparent or rational reason, one brother can consider another brother his enemy, never resolving his feelings, but always acting on those irrational feelings.

2. Some people are born with a generosity and natural sweetness which seem to belie their upbringing: They are consistently forgiving and caring.

3. Concentrating solely on ourselves leads to social and emotional isolation, but freely and generously caring for others enriches our lives.

4. Exerting unnecessary control on ourselves limits our choices and impedes our chances for personal fulfillment, whereas allowing ourselves the freedom to plunge into an uncontrolled, unpredictable environment offers more choices and, thus, more chances for happiness.

5. Our attitude toward food (nourishment) reveals much about our personalities: in what manner we provide food for ourselves or others; if we provide food for others; how we accept food from others. In other words, our habits of bodily nourishment may be equated with emotional and social nourishment.

6. When parents' behavior is irrational and unpredictable, the impact on their children is considerable. Often, however, parents are unaware of the consequences of their attitudes and actions, not only for present family harmony but also for their children's futures.

7. One family incident, a seemingly small or unnoticed event, can influence the future of a family; that incident may influence forever the course of action and subsequent feelings among family members.

- As you re-read the list of theses, select the one that you want to focus on as you read *Dinner at the Homesick Restaurant*.

- As you read the book, make marginal notes agreeing or disagreeing with, qualifying or refining, the initial statement that you selected.

- Use your notes to write a first-draft paper. Refine, reorganize, and personalize the initial statement.

Collect the papers and distribute them to different students in the class for peer editing.

- On a separate piece of paper, make comments as you edit your classmate's paper. Make suggestions for changes, but also acknowledge what you consider to be already well-written about the paper.

Collect the papers and return them to their authors.

- After you receive your edited paper, rewrite it, making necessary changes and clarifying what you have written. "All writing is rewriting."

COMMENTS

Presenting your students with model themes (theses) before the reading begins, shows them what a theme is, provides a valuable focus, and establishes a theoretical basis for personal reaction while reading. Once the model is worked through, from draft to peer review and discussion to final essay, a student refines and corrects the thesis. Students' work becomes original, and their ability to discover theme and formulate a thesis independently is strengthened.

Little House in the Big Woods
by Laura Ingalls Wilder

Source

Mielke, Nedra S. "Writing across the Curriculum as Applied in an Enrichment Classroom Setting." 1988. 11 pp. **ED 306 184**

and

Willingham, Terri Lynn. "Frontiers for Learning," *Learning*, v16 n6 Feb 1988, pp. 48-51.

Brief Description

Students participate in a simulation of an early pioneer, one-room school.

Objective

To experience learning according to our nostalgic imagination, the way it was done in the 19th century and on the frontier.

Procedures

Assign Laura Ingalls Wilder's book, *Little House in the Big Woods*.

- Research a typical day in a one-room school and write a one- or two-page summary.
- With assistance from your teacher, plan a special day during which you will simulate that typical day in a one-room school.

Some suggestions for your one-room school are these:

Teaching the 3 R's (using *McGuffey Readers*)

Stress the traditional values of courtesy, neatness, economy, obedience, respect, conversation, and kindness.

Girls wear skirts. They may wear pinafores, bonnets, aprons, and even long skirts of cotton, linen, or wool. Shoes are to be "sensible."

Boys can tuck trouser legs into long socks to make knickers. Corduroy pants or overalls are preferable to blue jeans. Plain colored or plaid flannel shirts would be appropriate. Shoes are to be "sensible" (not athletic shoes).

Pack a lunch basket, bag, or bandana with a brown-bread sandwich. The sandwich should be made with meat, egg salad, or cheese. Use apples, cold cornbread, and gingerbread or sugar cookies. (They could not get oranges [except at Christmas time] or bananas, or make chocolate chip cookies!)

Remember, they did not have paper napkins, soft drinks, or paper tissues.

Use pencils; they did not have ball-point or felt-tipped pens.

At recess, play the games that Laura enjoyed; several are mentioned in her books.

Have a spelling bee.

You might want to ask another grade to participate in this project with you. This would enable the students to get the feel of more than one grade being taught in the same room.

After the simulation, ask the students to write an essay giving their reactions to the project. Ask them to compare a one-room-school situation with their present school situation.

The Laura Ingalls Wilder series:

Little House in the Big Woods

Farmer Boy

Little House on the Prairie

On the Banks of Plum Creek

By the Shores of Silver Lake

The Long Winter

Little Town on the Prairie

These Happy Golden Years

The First Four Years

On the Way Home

West from Home: Letters of Laura Ingalls Wilder, San Francisco

LITTLE HOUSE IN THE BIG WOODS
BY LAURA INGALLS WILDER

SOURCE

Mielke, Nedra S. "Writing across the Curriculum as Applied in an Enrichment Classroom Setting." 1988. 11 pp. **ED 306 184**

BRIEF DESCRIPTION

Students identify the impact of the environment on the early settlers' ways of life, compare certain aspects of frontier and rural life to life today, and participate in writing activities related to the pioneer theme.

OBJECTIVE

To compare problems experienced by early pioneers in their everyday way of life to life now.

PROCEDURES

Assign Laura Ingalls Wilder's book, *Little House in the Big Woods*. Give your students a short biographical sketch of Laura.

BIOGRAPHY OF LAURA INGALLS WILDER

Laura Elizabeth Ingalls was born in Pepin, Wisconsin, on February 7, 1867, to Charles and Caroline Ingalls. "Pa" Ingalls had a pioneering spirit, and the family rarely stayed in one place for long. After leaving Pepin in 1868, they moved to Rothville, Missouri; Independence, Kansas; back to Pepin; on to Walnut Grove, Minnesota; Burr Oak, Iowa; and back to Walnut Grove. In 1879, they settled in De Smet, South Dakota.

Laura started teaching school in 1883, when she was 15 years old. Two years later she married Almanzo Wilder, who was 28. They had a daughter, Rose, and a son, who died in infancy. In 1894, Laura, Almanzo, and Rose settled in Mansfield, Missouri, at Rocky Ridge Farm.

Laura was 65 when she wrote her first book. Rose, an accomplished author, had persuaded her mother to write her memoirs. Laura's books describe in vivid detail her life as a pioneer. She tells of her close family ties, her adventures with her three sisters, and traveling across the vast prairie in a covered wagon. Her books paint a complete picture of the whole Ingalls family, including Pa, whose fiddle was never far from his side, and of Laura's older sister, Mary, who lost her eyesight at age 14.

Laura Ingalls Wilder died at Rocky Ridge Farm on February 10, 1957, three days after her 90th birthday. Almanzo had died in 1949 at age 92. Rose died in 1968.

PROJECT ONE: PIONEER HOMES

- Compare the homes of Laura Ingalls Wilder with homes today.
- Imagine that you are selling your homestead. Design advertisements to be posted, figure the selling price, and calculate the profit (or loss).
- Construct a mobile to illustrate aspects of an early settler homestead.

PROJECT TWO: ENVIRONMENT, HABITAT, AND HEALTH

- Write about the ways our lives are affected by the natural environment.
- Compare the immigration of people to the migration of birds and changes of habitat among animals for various reasons and purposes. Do some people migrate? What's the difference between "immigration," "emigration," and "migration?"
- Compare health practices of early settlements with those of today.

PROJECT THREE: PIONEER ACTIVITIES

- The word "pioneer" is used in the context of starting something new. Write about pioneers in an area such as science or politics or social arrangements.
- Write about the preservation and preparation of food during pioneer days.
- Write a pioneer ballad, and sing it to a familiar tune.

COMMENTS

Comparing a past way of life to the present helps students examine and understand change in the physical, social, and cultural environment, and factors that precipitate change.

Murder Mysteries
by Agatha Christie

Source

Hardesty, Susan M. "Using the 'Little Grey Cells,'" *English Journal*, v72 n5 Sep 1983, pp. 37-41.

Brief Description

Students complete lessons in language study, dialects, metaphoric language, creative writing and dramatization, reasoning skills, and composition/reasoning-skill activities.

Objective

To use Agatha Christie's appeal to spark students' interest in reading and literary appreciation, creative writing, language study, and reasoning skills.

Procedures

Language Study

Translate British English into American English

1. "Someone in the house was in this—one of the servants. I had them all up, blackguarded them right and left. They never split on each other.... Finally, I lost my temper and sacked the whole bunch."

2. Third floor flat.

3. "...it's my cousin Gladdie...she's *lost her place*."

Dialects

Read the passage aloud for phonetic meaning, then translate into Standard American English. Finally, capture some of your own dialect in a similar note.

Dear Mister:

You're the lawyer chap wot acts for the young feller. If you want that painted foreign hussy showd up for wot she is in her pack of lies you come to 16 Shaw's Rents Stepney to night. Itull cawst you 2 hundred quid. Arsk for Missis Mogson.

Novels

METAPHORIC LANGUAGE

Start a discussion about the link between language and emotion.

1. "The reptilian old man, known in the press and the courses as a 'hanging judge'..."

2. "This town's a hotbed of gossip—a lot of scandalmongering old women get together and invent Heaven knows what. They read these scurrilous rags of newspaper, and nothing will suit them but that someone in their town shall get poisoned, too."

CREATIVE WRITING AND DRAMATIZATION

Build an original murder mystery around the nursery rhymes below:

Peter, Peter Pumpkin Eater
Had a wife, but couldn't keep her.
Put her in a pumpkin shell,
And there he kept her very well.

Baa, Baa, Black Sheep, have you any wool?
Yes, sir, yes, sir, three bags full.
One for my master, and one for my dame,
And one for the little boy who lives down the lane.

REASONING SKILLS

These brainteasers come directly from Christie plots. Remember that she often said that the simplest solution is the most obvious solution.

1. Why would the same person, Mr. M., be present at the scene of four different murders? He is not the murderer nor is he an investigator.

    Answer: He is being framed for the murders.

2. Why would airholes be cut in a trunk containing the body of a murdered man?

    Answer: The man was not dead when he got into the trunk.

COMPOSITION/REASONING SKILL ACTIVITIES

+ Pretend that you are the police officer who must submit the final, factual report on a murder case.

+ Read to a particular point in the story, then compose a solution.

+ Investigate the real-life parallels/references in a work (i.e., legal procedures, monetary system, ranks of nobility, etc.).

✦ Compare a film version of a novel with the original text's plot, characterization, setting, emotional effect, etc.

COMMENT

Two books that would be of help in teaching Agatha Christie's whodunits are these:

1. Gwen Robyns, *The Mystery of Agatha Christie* (New York: Doubleday, 1978).

2. Dick Riley and Pam McAllister, eds., *The Bedside, Bathtub, and Armchair Companion to Agatha Christie* (New York: Frederick Ungar, 1979).

Biography and Autobiography

Laura Ingalls Wilder

THE DIARY OF A YOUNG GIRL
BY ANNE FRANK

SOURCE

Powers, John. "Writing to Learn: The Diary of Anne Frank," *The Writing Notebook*, v7 n2 Nov/Dec 1989, p. 16-17.

BRIEF DESCRIPTION

Students use visual props, design posters, and complete a series of writing projects.

OBJECTIVE

To prepare students to study literature that can be controversial or upsetting because of its subject matter.

PROCEDURES

HISTORICAL PREPARATION

Students can be easily upset by movies depicting the great numbers of dead bodies piled up in concentration camps. One effective way to prepare students for the enormity of this atrocity is to use numbers in different ways to try to comprehend six million—6,000,000 murdered people!

Begin by stacking 10 poker chips on your desk, and then ask a student volunteer to measure the stack. With this information, ask the student to calculate the height of 100 chips, 1,000 chips, and so on up to six million.

As a homework assignment but without telling your students why they are doing it, ask them to make a poster illustrating 6 million in a visually understandable way. Some ideas: How long could one play a video game with six million quarters? How many jars would it take to hold six million dill pickles?

Next, ask your students visually to represent 6 million people. For instance, how many square feet of beach is needed to provide a spot in the sun for six million people?

Display all the posters. Now is the time to make the grim announcement: Six million was the number of Jews systematically killed during the Holocaust, besides Gypsies, Slavs, homosexuals, disabled people, and religious minorities.

There will be many questions. Be prepared to answer these questions. Refer interested students to the library, where they will find books and videos and a wealth of information on the Holocaust.

This is a good time to have students write their thoughts in journal form.

EMOTIONAL PREPARATION

Give each student a paper grocery bag. Explain that to avoid being sent to a concentration camp, many people went into hiding. Often they could take with them only what they could carry. As a homework assignment, ask your students to choose the items they would take into hiding. These items must fit into the grocery bag. They are not actually to fill the bag, but to list the objects on the bag.

After the students have shared their lists, have them write about the items that they could not fit into the bag, as well as the reasons for choosing the items that they did.

As a class, read the book *Diary of a Young Girl*. Throughout the reading, have your students pause, either to reflect on what they have read or to write in response to one of the following prompts.

WRITING PROMPTS

1. Before beginning the reading, have students write letters of farewell to best friends that they may never see again.

2. At the halfway point in the reading, have students write letters to the same friend, explaining daily life in the Annex, and what they miss most.

3. At various points in the reading, have them write interior monologues for different characters in specific dramatic scenes.

4. Occasionally, have students make diary entries that Anne might have written at a given point. Compare these entries with those from Anne's diary at the same point.

5. At the end of the reading, have students describe how they would spend the day with Anne if she could be transported from the book to the present.

THE DIARY OF A YOUNG GIRL
BY ANNE FRANK

SOURCE

Bonnici, Charles. T*eaching Literature Grade 9: Integrating the Communication Arts. The Biography Experimental.* New York City Board of Education, Division of Curriculum and Instruction, 131 Livingston Street, Room 613, Brooklyn, New York 11201. 1985. 76 p. **ED 290 152**

BRIEF DESCRIPTION

Students answer probe questions and keep a diary.

OBJECTIVE

Students will be able to compare and contrast Anne's life before and after her entry into the Annex, understand and describe the historical situation that forced the Franks into hiding.

PROCEDURE

Assign the reading of Anne Frank's, *Diary of a Young Girl*.

Make photocopies of the accompanying study guide to give to the students.

Biography and Autobiography

STUDY GUIDE TO
THE DIARY OF A YOUNG GIRL
BY ANNE FRANK

This guide is intended to provide some direction to your reading of Anne Frank's *Diary* and to give you some aids to assist you in your reading. Please finish reading this book by _____. Your "Diary" entries are due on _____. These entries will vary in length. The Diary Assignments below describe what type of entry you are to make in your own diary. Each entry must be at least 100 words in length.

LIST OF CHARACTERS

It is often difficult to keep track of who's who when the characters in a book have strange-sounding names. Keep the following list handy when you are reading. It will help you remember who's who in Anne's *Diary*.

1. Anne's friends before she goes into the Secret Annex
   - Lies Goosen, Sanne Houtman, Jopie de Wall—Anne's girlfriends and schoolmates
   - Mr. Keptor—one of Anne's teachers
   - Harry Goldberg—a boy Anne liked
   - Peter Wessel—a boy Anne liked, but who didn't pay her much attention

2. Inhabitants of the Secret Annex
   - Anne Frank—the writer of this diary
   - Margo Frank—Anne's sister, three years older than Anne
   - Mr. Otto Frank ("Pim")—Anne's father
   - Mrs. Mansa Frank ("Mummy")—Anne's mother
   - Mr. Van Daan ("Putti")—a business associate of Mr. Frank whose family joined the Franks in hiding
   - Mrs. Petronella Van Daan ("Kerli")—Mr. Van Daan's wife
   - Peter Van Daan—the Van Daans' teenage son
   - Mr. Albert Dussel—a dentist friend who later joins the refugees in the Annex

3. The Dutch people who helped the Franks
   - Mr. Kraler—manager of Mr. Frank's business firm
   - Mr. Koophius—an assistant manager of the firm
   - Miep Van Santen—an employee of the firm
   - Henk Van Santen—Miep's husband
   - Elli Vossen—a young typist, later engaged to be married
   - Mr. Vossen—Elli's father, who works in the warehouse

MOTIVATION

- In the past, there has been a good deal of talk about putting more restrictions on teenagers, such as a nighttime curfew and a requirement to carry a teenage I.D. card. Do you think that you need such laws to govern your behavior? Why or why not?

- Suppose some such law were passed (e.g., a curfew requiring all teenagers to be indoors by 9:00 p.m.). What would you do?

DEVELOPMENT

- What restrictions were placed on Anne's life in Holland?

- What background material can you find to help you understand the historical background of Anne's diary during the Holocaust years?

- How did Anne and her family react to anti-Semitic laws?

- What would you have done in her situation?

- What would have happened to you?

- What normal aspects of Anne's life continued in spite of the laws of the state? (school, boys, etc.)

- How did Anne's life change when her family entered the Annex?

SUMMARY

- Would you have gone into hiding like the Franks? Why or why not?

Biography and Autobiography

DIARY ASSIGNMENT

Keep a diary of your own. The following diary assignments correspond with the sections in the book.

1. In her entry of July 9, 1942, Anne describes the Secret Annex. For your diary entry, describe your house or apartment. You may draw a diagram, if you wish.

2. Anne described a number of quarrels in her diary. For your entry, describe a quarrel in which you yourself took part or that you witnessed.

3. Choose one of the assignments below:
   a. Anne can't get along with her mother. Write an entry in your diary in which you describe how you get along with either your mother or father.
   b. Anne writes, "I am surrounded by a great void," and explains what she means by this. Do you ever feel this way? If so, write a diary entry about it.

4. Anne takes the proverb, "Misfortunes never come singly," and explains how it applies to her situation. For your diary entry, select any common proverb (use Anne's, if you wish, or choose a different one), and explain how it applies to you and your present situation in life.

5. Anne describes a typical day in the Annex. Select one part of your day (morning or afternoon or evening) and describe it in your diary entry.

6. Anne describes her pen—how she received it, cherished it, and finally lost it. For your diary entry, write about something you value and cherish very much.

7. Anne's entries are describing what it feels like to fall in love for the first time. For your diary entry, describe how you felt the first time that you were in love.

8. Anne looks back over the past two years of her life and describes both the change in her circumstances and her growth as a person. For your diary entry, look back over the past two years of your life. Describe what has happened to you and how you've changed as a person.

9. Anne describes what her writing—her main hobby and hoped-for career—means to her. Describe your main interest and what it means to you.

10. Anne goes to her father for advice about Peter and their relationship. Father tells Anne exactly what he thinks. For your diary entry, describe an occasion when you went to someone else (it need not be a parent) for advice; describe the advice given, and whether or not you took it and why.

11. Anne uses her diary to confess to something she's done that she knows was wrong because it hurt someone she loved. For your diary entry, make a confession; describe how you hurt someone you loved and how you felt about it.

12. Anne reacts to a book she is reading by responding to, and criticizing, the author's ideas. For your entry, write your reaction to, and possible criticism of, Anne's diary.

THE STORY OF MY LIFE
BY HELEN KELLER

SOURCE

Holland, Barbara W. "A Study Unit About Helen Keller: The Miracle," G/C/T, n36 Jan-Feb 1985. p. 12-13.

BRIEF DESCRIPTION

Students complete a questionnaire, reading assignments, research assignments, creative-writing exercises, drama/public-speaking exercises, and complete a project.

OBJECTIVE

To increase students' empathy with the personal hardships and triumphs that handicapped persons experience in their daily lives.

PROCEDURES

QUESTIONNAIRE

Before they read Helen Keller's autobiography, ask each student to answer the following questions to elicit their attitudes toward the handicapped.

- What does "handicapped" mean?
- Have you ever considered yourself to be handicapped? When, how, and why?
- Have you ever avoided talking to, or associating with, a handicapped person?
- Do you have a handicapped friend or member of your family?
- Name five famous handicapped people.
- Who was Helen Keller?
- Why do some peope use the term "physically challenged" instead of "handicapped?" What other words can you think of that have been used to describe people with problems like these? Ask someone with severe difficulties what term(s) they prefer.

READINGS

Students begin their study by reading short, biographical essays about Helen Keller. A search through old textbooks probably would produce some very good examples, such as the following:

1. Brooks, Van Wyck, "Helen Keller," *Adventures for Readers*, Book I, 1963. pp. 292ff.

2. Keller, Helen, "A Word of Advice," *Adventures for Readers*, Book I, 1963. pp. 297ff.

3. Keller, Helen, "Helen Keller Discovers the World," *New Horizons*, Book II, 1964. pp. 314ff.

ASSIGNMENTS

RESEARCH

After your students complete the background reading and discuss what they have learned about Helen Keller, ask them to proceed with the following writing tasks:

- Write a business letter to one of the addresses listed with the article entitled "Handicapped" in the H volume of the *World Book Encyclopedia*. Ask for pamphlets or other kinds of information about handicapped persons.

- Make a display of the braille alphabet. Then write in braille, or translate into braille, a message of at least twenty words.

- Write one complete sentence defining each of these terms:
    a. Down's Syndrome
    b. Glaucoma
    c. Arthritis
    d. Cleft Palate
    e. Congenital Blindness
    f. Amblyopia
    g. Amputation
    h. Cerebral Palsy
    i. Prosthesis

- Find out how seeing-eye dogs are trained. After outlining what you have discovered, explain what you have learned in a brief report.

Creative Writing

- Pretend that you have just met Helen Keller. Write a letter to a friend telling your friend your impressions of Ms. Keller.

- Imagine yourself as a person with a severe handicap. Put yourself into a situation, then write a story about how you feel about others, and how they react to you.

- Borrow a wheel chair. Take turns spending a day—a whole day—at school in the wheel chair. Write about what it was like being handicapped at school.

Drama/Public Speaking

- Learn to "sign" your name and a simple sentence using American Sign Language. Take turns with a friend "signing" sentences and guessing their meanings. (See the chart of the American Sign Language on page 65.)

- With others of your group, prepare a panel discussion about famous handicapped persons. Each member of the panel is to choose a different individual and find out as much as possible about that person. Present your information in the format of a panel discussion, not as individual reports.

- Act out a scene from *The Miracle Worker* by William Gibson (1960), or *The Story of My Life* by Helen Keller (1954).

- With a friend or by yourself, prepare a project about Helen Keller, the physical senses, handicapped persons, or some other related subject. Use your imagination to think of something you can demonstrate or "show and tell."

Project Ideas

- Compile a scrapbook of newspaper and magazine items about handicapped people.

- Do library research to find out statistics on the handicapped, and prepare a report by designing graphs and charts.

- Assemble a glossary of technical terms and other special words about handicapped people (including the harsh and insensitive words that have been used to describe them). What difference does it make what we call someone or something?

- Visit an architect and get either a photocopy of plans or photographs of a building especially designed for ease of access by handicapped people. Design a "perfect building" for easy access by all kinds of handicapped people.

EVALUATION

Write a paragraph or two explaining how your feelings towards, and attitudes about, handicapped people have changed. Exchange your paragraph(s) with a classmate, and read what the other person has written. Talk it over.

THE STORY OF MY LIFE
BY HELEN KELLER

SOURCE

Women as Members of Communities. Third Grade Social Studies: Abigail Adams, Sarah Winnemucca, Helen Keller, Shirley Chisholm, March Fong Eu, [and] Carmen Delgado Votaw. National Women's History Project, P. O. Box 3716, Santa Rosa, CA 95402. 1985. 60p. ED 260 998

BRIEF DESCRIPTION

Students read a short biography, answer questions, engage in discussions, and participate in group activities.

OBJECTIVE

To help your students gain insight into life with a disability.

PROCEDURES

The following lesson may be used in conjunction with Helen Keller's *The Story of My Life*.

Helen Keller was a leader for disabled peoples' rights. She spoke out and informed many people about her life and the lives of other disabled people.

Ask your students to read the following short biography of Helen Keller.

HELEN KELLER
(JUNE 27, 1880-JUNE 11, 1968)

Can you imagine what it would be like if you couldn't see or hear anything at all? Absolutely nothing? Helen Keller was a healthy baby, but when she was almost two years old, she became very ill. After this sickness, she was deaf and blind. She grew like any other healthy child, but she lived in a world with neither sights nor sounds.

When she was six years old, Helen's parents took her to a famous eye doctor. After examining Helen, he told her parents that she would always be deaf and blind. They talked to many other doctors, trying to find someone who could help Helen. Finally, a doctor suggested that Anne Sullivan might help her. Anne turned out to be the very person Helen needed.

Anne was partially blind, and she had studied at a special school for six years. She knew how to use sign language for the deaf to teach Helen.

Six-year-old Helen did not know right from wrong. She could hear neither praise when she did something right nor scolding when she did something wrong. Her family had never disciplined Helen. They had indulged her because of her disabilities. Helen did not understand joy, happiness, and love. She did not understand what it was to laugh and play. She was angry most of the time. Anne had to help Helen learn how to behave. She needed to teach her how to get along with other people so she could enjoy life. How was Anne to do all this?

Anne began by teaching Helen that the things she wanted had names. In this way she would be able to ask for what she wanted, like a glass of water. Imagine not even being able to ask for a glass of water! When Helen would touch something, Anne would use the sign-language alphabet to spell the word into Helen's hand for her to feel. Helen's hand would copy Anne's finger motions, but Helen still did not know that the finger motions meant a word or a name. She did not know that things had names.

One night, something wonderful happened! Anne and Helen ate dinner with the family to show off how well Helen was learning her table manners. During the meal, though, Helen seemed to forget all she had learned. When Anne was trying to make her sit in her chair, Helen knocked over the water pitcher. Anne took Helen outside to fill the pitcher with water from the well.

As the water poured out from the pump, Anne kept spelling w-a-t-e-r into Helen's open hand. Suddenly a new look came over Helen's angry face. She understood what was going on! This thing had a name! Helen ran around excitedly, touching everything. She held out her hand to Anne to ask what other things were called. On that day, Helen started learning the names of things in the world.

Helen Keller grew up to be a remarkable woman. With her teacher's love and help, she accomplished many great things. Helen learned to read braille. She learned how to write. She learned how to speak clearly, which was very hard for her to do because she could not hear her own voice. She began to live an exciting life.

In her adult years, Helen earned her living by speaking in public. She talked to people all over the world. She told them about herself and how she had learned to do many things and how other people could learn just as she had done. She wrote many books, many newspaper articles, and much poetry. She joined the American Federation for the Blind and worked very hard for this organization. She visited many schools for the deaf and blind. She also went to homes for the physically disabled, giving them hope and encouragement for their futures.

Helen Keller's whole life was devoted to helping others and working with people who had disabilities, especially those like her own. She never stopped speaking and helping others. She had really learned how to enjoy life. She once said, "I cannot stop to grow old while there is so much work to do and so many children to help."

- What do you think is the most remarkable thing about Helen Keller?
- How did Helen Keller become deaf and blind?
- Who was the most important person in Helen's life?
- What was the first word that she understood?
- How did Helen earn a living as an adult?
- What would you miss the most if you were suddenly to lose your eyesight? Your hearing?
- What does the word "disabled" mean? How does someone become disabled? Do you know anyone with a disability? What do they have to do differently from you?

Activity 1

Divide the class into teams of twos and have them do an exercise in which one member of the team is deaf and blind (use ear plugs and blindfolds) and the other member serves as a guide. Provide different substances and objects to be felt and identified. Allow time for each team member to take a turn. Afterwards, have your students discuss their feelings and experiences. Complete the activity by having both students on a team write about their own feelings of what it was like both to be deaf and blind for even a short time and to be the guide of a blind and deaf person.

Activity 2

Have your class begin learning the sign language alphabet (photocopy the Sign Language alphabet on page 118 and give to your students). Start them by signing W - A - T - E - R.

Activity 3

Contact your local school district's Special Education department or the center for the disabled in your community. Request a speaker for the class. Ask for someone, preferably a woman, who will share her story with your students. Allow for plenty of time for your students to ask questions.

Activity 4

What services and organizations exist in your community for visually or hearing-impaired people? Have your students investigate your local situation, writing to learn more about the groups and services near you, and reporting their findings to the class. Some possibilities include the following:

For the Blind

Books for the Blind
Guide dogs
Braille Institute
Friends of the Blind
Department of Rehabilitation
Centers for Independent Living
Lions Club
Braille or taped books

For the Deaf

Canine Companions
T.D.D. (Telecommunications Device for the Deaf)
Department of Rehabilitation
Centers for Independent Living
Special crosswalk signals
Special telephone services

American Sign Language Alphabet

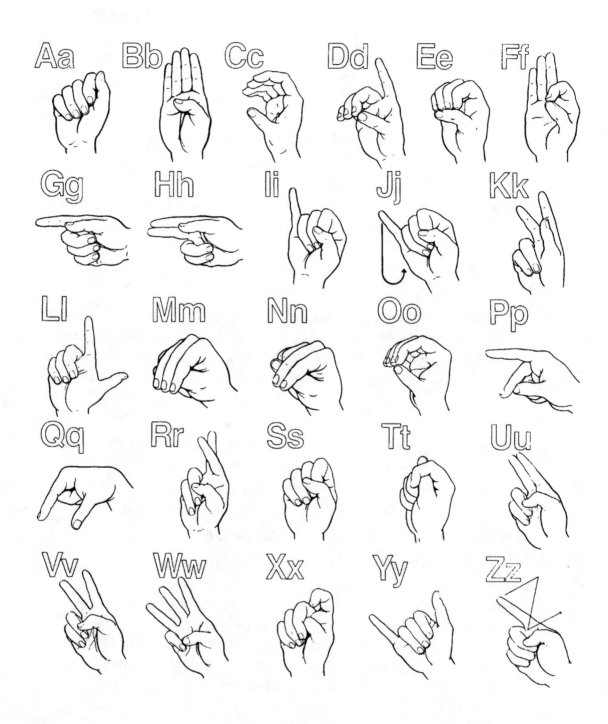

Kathy Weising, *Animals See & Sign*. (Orlando, Florida: See & Sign, Inc. 1989)
Illustration by Richard Sibley Associates, Inc., Orlando, Florida.
Copyright © 1989 by See & Sign, Inc. All Rights Reserved.

BIOGRAPHICAL DATA
JESSIE REDMON FAUSET AND MARY ROBERTS RINEHART

SOURCE

Waters, Bertha S., "Women's History Week in Pennsylvania. March 3-9, 1985." Pennsylvania State Department of Education, Harrisburg. 1984. 104pp. **ED 253 618**

BRIEF DESCRIPTION

A series of redesigned activities, originally conceived for younger students, using biographies of Jessie Redmon Fauset and Mary Roberts Rinehart.

OBJECTIVE

To make students aware that the lives of women authors influence their writing.

PROCEDURE

JESSIE REDMON FAUSET
1882-1961

During the 1920s, a group of actors, writers, musicians, poets, politicians, and other intellectuals was drawn to New York City where they settled in the uptown mecca called Harlem. Black people at that time were a tenth of the American population, so it was fitting that the influential Black leader, W.E.B. DuBois, referred to this extraordinary group as the "Talented Tenth." DuBois himself, Duke Ellington, Zora Neale Hurston, Langston Hughes, Claude McKay, Paul Robeson, Countee Cullen, and Charles Johnson were members of this cultural elite who contributed brilliantly to what is now known as the "Harlem Renaissance."

One of those who migrated to New York during this exciting decade was a young woman named Jessie Redmon Fauset. Novelist, poet, editor, and teacher, Jessie was the seventh child and fifth daughter of Anna and Redmon Fauset, from an old Philadelphia family. Jessie's father, whose forebears had lived in Philadelphia since the 1700s, was a minister in the African Methodist Episcopal Church. After Jessie graduated from the Philadelphia High School for Girls, her father's influence, together with her own superior academic abilities, won her admission to Cornell University. There she was elected to Phi Beta Kappa, possibly the first Black woman to receive that honor, and the first African-American to do so at Cornell. She graduated in 1905, pursued studies in French at the University of Pennsylvania, and received an M.A. in 1919.

Knowing about Jessie's life explains why her writing was once labeled "hopelessly genteel melodrama." As a child, she was permitted to read only the family Bible and Dante's *La Comedia Divina*. She was reared in a "very conservative, very religious household," by her own description. As a result, her essays described characters groomed in middle-class traditions. Her experiences also caused her to develop a burning social conscience and a passionate anger at the lives that most African Americans had to lead. She was not allowed to live in the dormitory at Cornell, and she had been rejected by Bryn Mawr because of her color. After college, she could not find a job in Philadelphia for the same reason.

Jessie taught French and Latin in Washington for 14 years while studying French at the Sorbonne each summer. Her occasional articles and book reviews were published in *The Crisis,* the journal of the NAACP edited by W.E.B. DuBois. As literary editor of *The Crisis,* she was able to showcase the work of young writers; she is credited with discovering Langston Hughes. Jessie's influence enabled female authors of the Harlem Renaissance to be published in the progressive children's magazine, *The Brownies' Book,* also edited by DuBois.

When her novel, *There Is Confusion,* was published in 1924, a diverse but distinguished company gathered to honor her at the Civic Club in New York City, including Eugene O'Neill, H. L. Mencken, Alain Locke, Gwendolyn Bennett, Nona Gale, Cullen and Hughes, as well as representatives of the major publishing houses. Fauset's other works include *Plum Bun* (1929), *Chinaberry Tree* (1931) and *Comedy: American Style* (1934).

Jessie Fauset taught French in a New York City high school from 1927 to 1944. She had married Herbert E. Harris in 1929, and they moved to Montclair, New Jersey, though Jessie continued to teach in New York. In 1949, she was a visiting professor at Hampton Institute in Virginia. Jessie Redmon Fauset died in Philadelphia in 1961.

MARY ROBERTS RINEHART
1876-1958

Mary Roberts Rinehart, best-selling author of crime novels, was born in Allegheny, Pennsylvania, the older of two daughters of Cornelia Grilleland and Thomas Beveridge Roberts. Mary Roberts's "abiding sense of sin" and her feeling that danger lurked in the midst of happiness, became components of her work, especially her crime novels.

When a woman doctor moved into their neighborhood, Mary envied the bag and buggy, symbols of a status that few women possessed. After she graduated from Allegheny High School at sixteen, however, her desire to go to medical school had to be postponed because of her youth and poverty. She enrolled at the Pittsburgh Training School for Nurses, where she faced a new world of industrial poverty and violence. The experience left her with "a terrible and often devastating pity and compassion" for the victims of society.

Mary graduated in 1896, the year after her father's suicide which deepened her sense of tragedy. In April 1896 she married Stanley M. Rinehart, a young surgeon. Three sons, Stanley, Jr.; Alan; and Frederick, were born during the next five years, and Mary became "an almost excessively devoted" mother. In 1903, when the family's security was threatened by stock market losses, she sat down to write at a rickety card table, and within a year she had sold forty-five stories. Her first published book was *The Circular Staircase* (1908). Mary produced sixty more books, but she consistently reiterated the primacy of her family over her writing.

Mary Roberts Rinehart served as a European correspondent in 1915 during World War I, toured camps in the United States as a representative of the Secretary of War, and returned to Paris to report the Armistice. *The Amazing Interlude* (1917) and *Dangerous Days* (1919) had heroines who fulfilled woman's true task as Mary saw it: Service. In *Bab: A Sub-Deb* (1917), a teenager, "tired of being told that the defense of our Dear Country is a masculine matter," breaks up an espionage ring to show the value of women in wartime.

Spending summers on a Wyoming ranch, Mary Rinehart became concerned about the plight of the Blackfoot Indians. She used her influence to raise money for them, even threatening an exposé in the *Saturday Evening Post*. In 1921, her husband resigned his post with the Veterans Bureau in Washington, D.C., in order to manage her business affairs. She had become a late convert to the cause of women's suffrage, convinced by arguments of economic equality. She wrote many pieces for magazines about the "New Woman," but she concluded that the world had changed more than women, and that the old roles were hard to fit into a new setting.

Mary Rinehart wrote several plays, among them the very successful *The Bat* (1920), coauthored with Avery Hopwood. A revival of *The Bat*, with Zasu Pitts, was filmed for television in 1953 after the play closed. Three movie versions were made; the last, in 1959, starred Agnes Moorehead.

After her husband's death in 1932, Mary Rinehart moved to New York City. In 1937 she covered the coronation of George VI, and during World War II she served as an air-raid warden. Ill health, serious accidents, several operations, and the tragic scalding death of her mother, intensified Mary's feeling that life offered no security. She finally became an Episcopalian, not so much because she believed in God but because she "was afraid He might exist and must be placated." After surgery for breast cancer, Rinehart courageously published her own story in the hope that it would help frightened women ("I Had Cancer," *Ladies' Home Journal,* July 1947). When she died in her sleep in New York in 1958, she left the manuscript of a personal memoir of her girlhood entitled "To My Sons."

Mary Roberts Rinehart was said to have been on the best-seller lists longer and more often than any other American author. The heroines of her stories are interesting women for whom murder and war are synonyms for liberation. Violence jolted the hide-bound spinster and repressed maiden into action and responsibility. Rinehart believed that women accomplished more than men, although the women never took themselves so seriously as did the males.

The happy endings in her stories were required by her conviction that optimism is central to American life, by her refusal to depress her children, and by her editors' demands. "I am frankly a story teller," she said in 1917. "Some day I may be a novelist." When her sons founded their own publishing firm, Rinehart felt that she "owed them a best seller" every year, and so the serious work she hoped to accomplish was left undone. The power of her writing was such that after *The Man in Lower Ten* (1909) was published, railroad passengers avoided that bunk for years, and Mary received fan letters from readers as diverse as Theodore Roosevelt and Gertrude Stein.

Biography and Autobiography

ACTIVITY 1

Invite a woman who works in a job not traditional for women to share her experiences with your class. Have your students prepare interview questions in advance. These might include asking her about the training required for her job, why she became interested in this type of work, what she especially likes about the job, what her dislikes are, and what she plans concerning her future working life.

You might introduce your special guest by having the students guess her occupation. Do not tell them that she holds a job untraditional for women. As they play a game of "Twenty Questions" or "What's My Line," your students may reveal to themselves their own gendered assumptions in the questions they ask the guest.

ACTIVITY 2

- Collect pictures and articles from newspapers, magazines, and advertisements showing women in traditional and non-traditional activities.
- Which are the easiest to locate?
- Do you know women involved in these activities?
- Write a short story based on someone you know in a non-traditional activity.

ACTIVITY 3

- Read the biographies on Jessie Redmon Fauset and Mary Roberts Rinehart.
- Write news releases on each author for radio or television to report the facts of a specific, important event. Pretending that the event has just happened, tell all of the important details—who, what, when, where, why, and how. Include a "grabber" attention-getting title or first line for the story. You might want to examine current news sources for articles concerning women who are presently working to change conditions for themselves and others.

Activity 4

- Conduct research on women and their work in any other specific time periods that you may choose. Topics to consider include the following:

    1. The varied jobs done by women in the early American colonies. (Include all kinds of women: Europeans and women from the British Isles, Africans and African-Americans, Latin Americans, Native Americans.)

    2. Immigrant women in the 19th century: Include where they came from, why they emigrated, where they worked, the condition of their lives.

    3. The lives of the Indian women of the tribe that lived nearest to your community, people whose descendents may still be your neighbors. (Not all Indians live in tipis and wear feathers! Many African-Americans are also part Native-American. Ask!)

    4. The work of migrant women, past and present.

    5. The women of Mexico and the West, before and after the Europeans arrived.

    6. Women workers in the garment industries, from the 1850s to the present.

    7. Women's roles during the major war periods and after.

Activity 5

- Brainstorm with your class to develop a list of questions to ask the older women who raised them about their lives. Help your students organize the questions into topics, or clusters of ideas, and then develop an appropriate questionnaire. Guide the discussion toward including questions related to the impact of the general historic events of the women's lives, migrations of their families, family expectations for females and males, attitudes about women's public lives.

- Using your questionnaire results, write an essay on the life of the woman you interviewed.

- Make public your report by reading it aloud to the class.

Comment:

The ERIC source gives biographical material on many other important women in U. S. history. You may obtain Waters's work through the ERIC system.

Short Stories

Maya Angelou

"My Man Bovanne"

by Toni Cade Bambara

Source

Davis, James E. "Re-Writing Bambara's 'My Man Bovanne.'" In Dorothy Matthews, ed., *Writing Assignments Based on Literary Works*. Illinois Association of Teachers of English, Urbana, Illinois. 1985. 76 pp. **ED 255 923**

Brief Description

Students rewrite a short story from a different perspective and then compare their version to the original.

Objective

To help students see the literary quality of a short story.

Procedures

- Read Toni Cade Bambara's short story, "My Man Bovanne."
- In your journal, rewrite the short story, choosing one of the following ideas:
    1. Tell the story from the point of view of one of Hazel's children.
    2. Re-write the story using an omniscient point of view.
    3. Turn Hazel into a White woman, and give her a White middle-class dialect.
    4. Tell a similar story with the Hazel character changed to a male.
    5. Summarize the story.
- Writing in your journal, compare your version of the story to the original. Comment on the difficulty you had in writing your version.

Comments

"My Man Bovanne" is a well-crafted, tightly written story that depends almost completely on the voice of its first-person narrator—her Black dialect, vocabulary, accent, wit, timing, instinct, and common sense—for its special humor and thought-provoking impact.

"PAUL'S CASE"
BY WILLA CATHER

SOURCE

Bodmer, Paul. "The Reader's Notebook: A Tool for Thinking with Writing." Paper presented at the Annual Meeting of the Conference on College Composition and Communication, 1990. 21 p. **ED 218 014**

BRIEF DESCRIPTION

Students participate in formal academic discourse by writing reaction papers, and they participate in informal writing by keeping a notebook of responses.

OBJECTIVE

To help students become active readers, and to make them active participants in the process of the story.

PROCEDURES

Ask your students to read a story by Willa Cather before the next class. When the students arrive in class the next day, ask them to open their notebook to the first blank page.

- Write the name of the story, the author's name, and the date on the blank page of your notebook.

- Start writing about the story. Write anything you want, but keep writing until you are asked to stop. If you can't think of anything to write about the story, then write, "I can't think of anything to write about this story." Repeat it, if necessary.

Allow the students to free-write for ten minutes.

- Read what you have written. Write a summation sentence that contains the most interesting, predominant, or intriguing idea, or the direction in which you think you are going.

Lead a class discussion, asking your students what they wrote about the story. Say nothing yourself about the story, only let the students share their responses.

Assign Willa Cather's story, "Paul's Case," to be read before the next class. Moreover, ask your students to free-write about the story before they come to class.

When they come to class, ask them to share what they have written. Let them ask questions, but do not answer them. Let the students discuss the questions among themselves, forming their own ideas.

- Open your notebook to your entry on this story. Using the summation sentence from this entry as a starting place, begin writing again.

- Write for ten minutes. Write a summation sentence.

- Share what you have written with the class.

- Now, write for another ten minutes. Write a final summation sentence.

Again, ask your students to share what they have written about their story and what the writing process revealed to them.

Using the notebook entries, ask your students to write a formal response to "Paul's Case."

"A Last Day in the Field"

by Caroline Gordon

Source

Oplt, Toni. "Caroline Gordon's 'A Last Day in the Field': Reading, Thinking, and Writing." In Dorothy Matthews, ed., *Writing Assignments Based on Literary Works*. Illinois Association of Teachers of English, Urbana, Illinois. 1985. 76 pp. **ED 255 923**

Brief Description

Students complete written responses to the story; with the aid of peer groups, they go through the steps of pre-writing, writing, and revision.

Objective

To teach students about writing as a process.

Procedures

Responses

Prepare a response page for students to complete as a homework assignment. The response page contains very general, open-ended questions about the text and the student's response to it. Ideally, students should fill out these responses either while they read the story or immediately after finishing it.

You may draw some of the questions for the response page from the following:

"A Last Day in the Field"

- It is not always obvious to the reader that Aleck dies at the end of the story, but he does. He has been warned by his doctor and his wife that going out hunting is dangerous for him because he is ill. It ends up costing him his life. Why do you think he decided to go? Was it a stupid or smart thing to do? Explain your answer.

- At the beginning of the story, Joe is inexperienced and neglectful (i.e., he shoots too soon and forgets to bring straw for the dogs), whereas

Aleck is a mature father-figure. How does that situation change by the end of the story? Give some examples.

- Do you know anyone who reminds you of Aleck or Joe? What, specifically, does the person you have in mind have in common with the characters in Gordon's story?

- Your homework assignment is to read Caroline Gordon's "A Last Day in the Field" and fill out the response page before coming to class.

CASES

Discuss your students' responses in class. This discussion will enlarge the frame of reference within which the students can write essays later.

Hand your students a page of "cases." These will provide structure for the writing assignments, for they are much more specific and detailed than the response questions. The idea in this case study is to provide an audience with a natural reason for writing, and a mode of communication for the writer.

Because it is possible, and perhaps desirable, to make cases complex, it is probably better to have students work in small groups. In the groups, the students are to review the cases, select one, discuss it as a group, and take notes.

REVISIONS

Ask your students to work in writers' circles: to engage in peer critique and revision preparatory to rewriting.

- One at a time, read your essays aloud to your group.

- Reread each essay in your group, filling out the revision questionnaire for each. Be honest in each evaluation. Sign each questionnaire and give it to the author of the essay.

"A Last Day in the Field" Cases

- You are Joe (or Joanna), and you have just come home from the hospital. When Aleck fell in the field, you had run to a nearby farmhouse to telephone for an ambulance. It was, of course, too late; Aleck died. You are very upset and are having a hard time talking to your parents and some nosey neighbors about what happened, yet you still need to explore your feelings. You decide to write about this "last day in the field" in your journal. You feel compelled to go over your memories of Aleck, of the times the two of you spent together—what he taught you about growing up. You also need to express your feelings about Aleck's decision to go hunting when he knew he shouldn't. Keep in mind that his last day was spent with you. Why did he choose to take the risk? Are you angry at him, or sad, or confused? Express your emotion.

- It has been a month since Aleck died. Some of the people in your town have been gossiping about Aleck, calling him stupid or careless—neglectful of other people's feelings (his wife's, for instance), or even sinful. Some equate his going hunting with committing suicide. You are outraged that Aleck's so-called friends are saying such horrible things about him. You decide to write a letter to the editor of your small-town paper telling them all what Aleck was really like—maybe you think he was brave or wise in his decision. Explain what he meant to you—what he taught you about living. You feel strongly about this, but you want your essay to be published, so you must write accordingly; perhaps a more formal tone is necessary here. Grammar and clarity will, of course, be very important.

- Maybe you do know someone like Aleck or Joe. Maybe they remind you, in different ways, of yourself. Have you ever had an experience like the one in the story? Describe the situation. Tell who was involved and what they said. Make it clear why this situation is important to you.

- What about suicide? What do you think, and how do you feel, about it? Can you use Gordon's story as an example to make your position on this subject clear? Be sure to back up all your claims with examples. Caution: This could involve research!

- **Your homework assignment** is to use the notes you wrote in your group discussion and begin writing an essay. This will be a first draft. Bring it to class tomorrow and we will make a copy for each person in your group.

Revision Questionnaire
"A Last Day in the Field"

1. Depending on which case was chosen, did the essayist use examples, details, a certain tone or vocabulary, to fullest potential? How could any of these have been better employed?

2. Did the essayist seem to have a sense of audience? Was the essayist convincing to that audience?

3. If the essayist had to take on a persona, was that convincing? What was believable? What was not? How could the essayist make it more believable?

4. In general, what was the organization of the essay? Was it easy to follow? If not, specifically tell where you became lost and why. What could the essayist do to make the essay more clear?

5. What are the essay's most serious flaws?

6. What are the essay's best qualities?

7. What did you like best and least about the essay?

Signature_____

✦ Using these critiques from your peers, rewrite a final draft of your own essay.

"THE LOTTERY"
BY SHIRLEY JACKSON

SOURCE

Henson, Leigh. "Discovering Theme through Writing: A Response-Oriented Approach to 'The Lottery.'" In Dorothy Matthews, ed., *Writing Assignments Based on Literary Works*. Illinois Association of Teachers of English, Urbana, Illinois. 1985. 76 pp. **ED 255 923**

BRIEF DESCRIPTION

Students use journal writing to complete two writing exercises.

OBJECTIVE

Enable students to exercise their attitudes and values in choosing a subject for journal writing; plan multi-paragraph formal composition.

PROCEDURES

Assign the reading of Shirley Jackson's short story, "The Lottery."

- Complete the following exercise in your journal, developing ideas completely and clearly. Use paragraphing as needed.

- Describe what you consider to be an important discovery, action, or reaction of a character or speaker in the story.

- What "statement" was Jackson making? State whether you agree or disagree and explain why. Support your view with specific information from the reading. Be alert for facts in the reading that might, however, lead you to alter your position or even change your subject.

- Tell what you think your analysis shows to be a truth about human nature or society.

Divide the class into small groups and ask them to discuss their journal entries. Suggest that they check whether their group members have used facts from the literature in their writing accurately and completely.

- Developing ideas completely and clearly, and using paragraphing as needed, write a sequel to the story in your journal.

- ✦ Think of an important discovery, action, or reaction of a character or speaker in the story.

- ✦ Describe a new scene—including dialogue, if you wish—that shows what you believe will be the most significant effect of that discovery, action, or reaction.

- ✦ Using facts only from the literary text, not your sequel, tell why you agree or disagree with the characters or speaker in that scene. Be alert to facts in the reading that might lead you to alter your sequel.

- ✦ Tell what you think your sequel shows as a truth about human nature or society.

Have the same small groups to review and discuss what their colleagues have written in their journals.

COMMENTS

A shift of emphasis in students' writing about literature, from *testing* them to developing their ability to *interpret,* is gratifying to them, more pleasant for you to grade, and reveals as much, or more, than do old-fashioned tests. These exercises for writing not only guide students towards interpretation of theme in a work of fiction or drama but also serve as a pre-writing activity for multi-paragraph formal composition.

"THE LOTTERY"
BY SHIRLEY JACKSON

SOURCE

Finkle, Sheryl L. "Teaching Shirley Jackson's 'The Lottery': A Sensitizing Approach." In Dorothy Matthews, ed. *Writing Assignment Based on Literary Works*. Illinois Association of Teachers of English, Urbana, Illinois. 1985. 76 pp. **ED 255 923**

BRIEF DESCRIPTION

Students complete a series of formal handouts prior to reading the story, while reading the story, and after reading the story. Using the information that they have gleaned from these assignments, they write essays, edit their peers' essays, and complete final drafts of their own essays.

OBJECTIVE

To develop writing skills using background information and formal devices.

PROCEDURES

1. Assign the reading of Shirley Jackson's short story, "The Lottery." To set the background for the story, ask your students to skim the text and complete the "Think before You Read!" handout.

2. Ask your students to read the story and complete the "Act While You Read!" handout.

3. After the students have finished reading the story, ask them to complete the "Re-Think What You Read!" handout.

4. Explore your students' answers to the questions in the "Re-Think What You Read!" handout. Engage your class in a discussion of further questions they might have.

    With the re-thinking exercise still fresh in their minds, ask your students to write an essay about some idea in the piece of literature they have just studied. Ask them to list all they know about their topic as it is presented in the story, and then draw connections between that information and information from their own experience.

Collect the essays and then redistribute them to the class, making sure that no one gets his or her own paper. Ask your students to edit the essays with special emphasis on elaboration of detail, logical structure of ideas, and the degree of predictability established for the reader.

After the essays have been returned to their authors, ask your students to study their peer editor's comments, and then draft a final revision of their essays.

COMMENT

The value of these activities is that they posit a strategy for students to use when making connections among ideas, and subsequently in structuring those ideas so that meanings in the texts they read and write become focused and communicable.

Short Stories

THINK BEFORE YOU READ!

1. The title of Shirley Jackson's story is "The Lottery." What is a lottery? What can you predict about what will happen in the story, based on this knowledge?

2. Shirley Jackson sometimes wrote stories that were bizarre or terrifying. List the details from the first paragraph of the story. Do these details seem consistent with what we have been told about Jackson's stories? What does this information from the text suggest to you about the story?

3. We are told that this story has something to do with what we know about people in this small town. As you skim the text, list the first five names you encounter. Do these names seem typical to you? Based on this observation, can you predict that this story is talking about real-life characters?

4. An objective narrator, like the one in this story, tells the story by reporting action and quoting dialogue. Answer the following questions about narration based on what you observe in the text.

   a. Roughly how much of the text appears to be action?

   b. How much of the text involves dialogue?

   c. Explain the patterns that these devices occasion in the text. Do you see long passages of action or long passages of dialogue? Which comes first? Are the action and dialogue mixed?

ACT WHILE YOU READ!

SECTION ONE

1. There is basically one action taking place in the first three paragraphs of the story. In light of this activity, what would you entitle the first section?

2. List in order of their appearance in the text the groups of characters who engage in this action.

3. List two details that the author gives about each group.

4. What do these details suggest to you about the people gathered?

SECTION TWO

5. What is the subject matter of the next set of four paragraphs?

6. Consider the paragraph about the original paraphernalia. What object is the central focus of this paragraph?

7. What kind of information are we given about this object?

8. The box and the slips of paper are a central part of this ritual. List several things you learn about them in the third paragraph of this section. For instance, slips of paper were substituted for wood chips to make room for more names. Does this remind you of any similar event in your own life? What do these details suggest about the people's attitude towards the lottery?

9. Describe some of the "fussing" that was done to prepare for the lottery. How have these details changed over the years? Do all of the people know what needs to be done to prepare and conduct the lottery? Why?

Short Stories

10. What questions have you developed about the story at this point? How have your first impressions or beliefs about the story changed?

SECTION THREE

11. Section three of the story parallels in its content one of the earlier sections. What section does it resemble and how are the sections alike?

12. To what one character are we introduced in this section? Are there any details that suggest that this woman is special?

13. How would you describe the feelings suggested by the following details about Mrs. Hutchinson?
    - her sweater over her shoulder
    - "Clean forgot what day it was."
    - people separated good-humoredly
    - "Wouldn't have me leave m'dishes in the sink?"

SECTION FOUR

14. What action takes place in the fourth section of the story? What title does this suggest for the section?

15. How does the amount of description and dialogue in this section compare with other parts of the story? How would you account for the differences?

16. How would you characterize the change in people's feelings in this section? Cite two specific examples or quotations from the text that indicate why you made this decision.

17. State briefly the procedure followed in conducting the lottery. What devices in the text stretch out these steps and yet keep your interest as each family draws from the box?

18. Several words in this section are italicized. Copy down the sentences in which you find these words, and briefly explain their significance.

Section Five

19. One might entitle the final section "The Act."
    What takes place here to suggest that title?

20. The children, along with their parents, pick up stones. Where earlier in the text did you observe this action? What were the children doing with the stones earlier? Contrast your understanding of their action now with your understanding at the time it was first mentioned. What did you think it meant then? What do you think it means now?

21. Several sentences indicate the willingness of all these people to cast stones. What details stand out as surprising, considering that Mrs. Hutchinson is the victim?

22. How does the description of the town in this final section contrast with the opening one? What questions are you left with at the end of the story? How has your first impression of the story been revised through your reading?

Re-think What You Read!

One device used in this story to hold our interest and emphasize the author's main point is irony (expecting one thing to happen but experiencing its opposite). To observe and understand irony, we sometimes have to see an object or statement two different ways at the same time.

As you complete the questions below, consider Shirley Jackson's use of parts of her story to foreshadow or warn us of the irony.

1. Reconsider the first paragraph of the story. Given the details there, did you expect the lottery to be a happy occasion or a grim one? Why did you make that decision? Knowing the outcome of the story now, what details seem ironic in that paragraph? Explain.

2. The names in the story are realistic; they describe ordinary people. Is there anything about these names that points to the ironic nature of the story as well? List the names that might be considered two ways at once. Tell what significance the name has to the story. For instance, a martin is a bird associated with bringing bad news.

3. When Mrs. Hutchinson arrives, she greets Mrs. Delacroix in a particular way. Write the sentence that describes this action; indicate why it might be significant.

4. Consider the sections into which we divided the story. Diagram the action of "The Lottery," indicating whether the action is in the past or present, internal or external.

5. Write a paragraph in response to one of the following question sets. Use specific details from the text, as we have done in the questions above, to support the opening statement of your response.

   a. The introduction to this story suggests that "The Lottery" is a comment on something we know about each other and something we know about how evil works. After having read the story, what would you say is the something we know about how evil works in ordinary people?

   b. "The Lottery" is a persuasive nightmare. Do you agree? Why? Consider the military draft or some other real-life experience along with some samples from the text to determine your answer.

   c. "The Lottery" is an example of the destructive power of merely accepting a situation because "that's how things used to be" or because "that's the way things are." Explain what people mean by such statements. Support your explanation with details about one or two significant characters and their attitudes and actions in the text.

"How I Contemplated the World from the Detroit House of Correction and Began My Life Over Again"

by Joyce Carol Oates

Source

Dorley, Sandra. "Joyce Carol Oates and Body Sculpture: Using Family Counseling to Teach Literature," *Teaching English in the Two-Year College,* v17 n4 Dec 1990.

Brief Description

Students use body sculpture to become full participants in their own exploration of modern fiction. They follow up the body sculpture exercise with a written essay.

Objective

Students better understand the complex relationships between characters and the part those relationships play in motivation; their participation in class is increased; they begin to consider their own family relationships.

Procedures

Joyce Carol Oates's short story, "How I Contemplated the World from the Detroit House of Correction and Began My Life Over Again," has choppy structure, and the initial confusion in this story makes it difficult for many students to read and understand.

The use of the body sculpture helps students to discover what the story is saying.

While body sculpture has been used in speech classes, it is a new and useful technique for teachers of literature/composition. Combining elements of drama with psychological evaluation, body sculpture enables students to become full participants in their own exploration of modern fiction. They are able to demystify this type of story by gaining valuable insight into the underlying motivations of fictional characters.

BODY SCULPTURE

Body sculpture was developed by Virginia Satir in the late 1960s "to help family members become more aware of self in relation to their own families." The goal of this visual structuring is to help each family member improve family membership and relationships, and to bring the family to a better understanding of members' needs.

Family shaping begins in a counseling session when one member of the family, such as a daughter, is selected to "shape" the entire family group. She does this by asking each family member to take a position in a living tableau that she "sculpts" in the counselor's presence. Persons in her family with whom she feels an emotional closeness tend to be placed closer in the tableau, whereas those who are distant emotionally are placed physically distant. Very often, the "sculpture" being shaped will have the members kneeling, reaching with outstretched arms, turning their backs to other members of the family, or any number of other meaningful postures. The total effect enables the counselor and the family graphically to see how the one doing the shaping believes she fits into the family structure. It also shows her perceptions of the rest of the family members' relationships with each other.

For example, if the second-born daughter believes that she is not so close to her mother as the first-born son, she will place the son closer and herself farther away. If the father feels removed from the family, for whatever reason, he may place himself at one side of the room and the rest of the family grouped together on the other side.

The counseling session concludes with both counselor and family members discussing their perceptions of what has been "sculpted." Virginia Satir believed that "one advantage of sculpture is that, as a behavioral demonstration, it is much more accurate in what it reflects about family communications than a verbal description."

The strength of this technique—the comment it makes on the interrelationships of the family members—is the main reason that it is also effective as a means of teaching short fiction. Characterization is integral to literary analysis, and students often ignore fiction's mirroring of life; they view stories, instead, as fictions outside of the realm of their own, real experience. Helping readers to see connections with reality improves their understanding of the text.

CLASSROOM APPLICATION

Before you ask your students to read Oates's "House of Correction," as a pre-reading activity suggest that they write down thoughts about their own families, the relationships among the members within them, and their perceptions of how they themselves fit into the family structure.

Inform your students that they are going to examine Oates's story in a way completely different from the usual classroom discussion of literature. Tell them about family body sculpture. Using several members of your class as characters, demonstrate the technique by sculpting your own family relationships. This models the sculpting process for the students in a non-threatening manner. Once body sculpture has been explained and demonstrated, you can begin discussing the story.

Make certain that your students see that the action of the story takes place in four distinct settings, and that these sections correspond to acts in a play. To participate in sculpting the action, divide your class into four groups, one for each of the four basic scenes in the story. Give instructions as follows:

- Each group is to work with one of the four acts.

- Decide which scene to use and what characters you will include in the tableau.

- Discuss the characters and their relationships to each other.

- You have 5 to 10 minutes to plan your tableau.

- Present your scenes to the rest of the class in the same order in which they occur in the story.

- Tell which scene you have chosen and explain why.

- If there are not enough members in a group to portray all of the characters needed, then draw on classmates from other groups to fill out the scene.

Once a group has arranged itself in tableau, you may question them about why they sculpted the scene as they did. Ask about their choices and the decisions that informed the arrangement. Call on them to justify their tableau by reference to the text of the story.

After a group finishes staging the tableau, and you have questioned them about the spatial relationships portrayed, reserve time for questions or responses from other class members directed to the group sculptors. Remind everyone to justify their interpretation of their body sculptures with textual references.

It is a good idea to allow a few minutes at the end of the class for you to clear up any remaining questions regarding the story. Because this story is rather difficult, and because body sculpture is an unfamiliar technique to most students, it may be difficult to complete staging all four of the scenes in one fifty-minute class.

The whole experience can be concluded with a writing assignment based on questions generated by the story and the body sculptures. These topics can be adjusted to the literacy and maturity of your students.

"A Visit of Charity" and "A Worn Path"

by Eudora Welty

Source

Sasse, Mary. "Peas, Honey, and Eudora Welty." In Dorothy Matthews, ed. "On Contemporary Literature: Critiques, Reviews and Recommendations." Illinois Association of Teachers of English, Urbana, Illinois. 1985. 66 pp. **ED 252 860**

Brief Description

Students describe a visit to the sick and elderly; they read "A Visit of Charity"; they write an interior monologue; they read "A Worn Path"; they write a summary essay.

Objective

To discover similarities between personal experiences and what is read.

Procedures

As a pre-reading activity for the two stories, ask your students to describe in writing a visit to a nursing home, an elderly relative's house, or a hospital/clinic. Ask them to tell why they went; to describe what they saw, heard, and smelled; to describe the people they met; and to remember and relate how they felt on leaving.

Immediately after finishing the pre-reading activity, ask your students to read "A Visit of Charity."

Ask your students to write an interior monologue from the point of view of one of the old ladies, beginning with Marian's entrance into the room. Or they may write from the nurse's point of view as she views both Marian and the old ladies.

Before reading "A Worn Path," ask your students to think about the following advice for readers, based on Barbara Pannwitt, *The Art of Short Fiction* (Boston: Ginn, 1964), pp. 20-21:

- Read for pleasure. Get to know the characters as people, responding favorably or unfavorably to them, fearing for them, enjoying their success, sympathizing with them in their defeats, approving or disapproving of their actions.

- Notice what is happening. Try to remember as many of the details as possible.

- Inhabit the world of the story, where and when it is taking place (both physically and psychologically), and adapt to its atmosphere and timing.

- Think about your own attitudes and expectations. Reflect on how you feel about the story.

- Ask yourself what important impressions you have received. They may or may not be what the author hoped they would be, but your perceptions on the basis of the evidence may bring forth ideas that the author never imagined.

Ask your students to read "A Worn Path" in class.

Prompt a class discussion of the differences, similarities, mood, imagery, point of view, irony, setting, and characterization in the two stories. After the discussion, ask your students to write an essay discussing these points of comparison.

COMMENTS

Setting up a reading situation helps students take an "inward journey," as Ms. Welty points out, "that leads us through time—forward or back, seldom in a straight line, most often spiraling. Each of us is moving, changing, with respect to others. As we discover, we remember; remembering, we discover; and most intensely do we experience this when our separate journeys converge. Our living experience at those meeting points is one of the charged dramatic fields of fiction." (*One Writer's Beginnings,* p. 102)

POETRY

Emily Dickinson

SWEET RHYMES

BY DOROTHY ALDIS

SOURCE

de Fina, Allan. "Sweet Rhymes by Dorothy Aldis," *Instructor,* v101 n7 March 1992, pp. 48-49.

BRIEF DESCRIPTION

Students read poems, participate in class discussion, learn about rhyming patterns, make collages, and write poetry.

OBJECTIVE

To study the poetry of Dorothy Aldis, and to learn about rhyming patterns.

PROCEDURES

Read the following short biography of Dorothy Aldis to your students:

Dorothy Keeley Aldis was born on March 13, 1896, in Chicago, Illinois. Her father was the managing editor of the *Chicago Tribune*.

As a child, Dorothy always loved to write. When she left college at age 19 and returned to Chicago, she applied for—and got—a job at her father's newspaper. Because Dorothy had used a false name to apply for the job, however, she worked for her father's company for many months before he discovered that she was his employee!

In 1922, Dorothy married Graham Aldis, and she gave birth to four children. Then, at mid-life, Dorothy began to write poetry. Recalling those days, she later explained that she had made time to write by driving to a deserted road. There, she would pull her car over and then pound away at the typewriter keys with her typewriter on a pad on her knees.

Dorothy Aldis's first book of poems, *Everything and Anything,* was published in 1925. During the following 40 years, she published 27 other books of poetry, teenage fiction, and nonfiction, as well as many magazine articles. Dorothy Aldis was given the Children's Reading Round Table Award posthumously in 1966.

Poetry

- Read the two poems by Dorothy Aldis on page 152.
- If you were going to write a poem about candy, what kinds of things would you say in it?
- What kinds of words could you use to make the poem sound delicious?
- Listen closely for the words that tell how to eat the different candies.
- Is there anything else that is special about some of the words the poet uses?
- "Onomatopoeia" is the word that says that words sound like the actions they describe. "Crunch"—the sound of teeth chewing; "slurp"—the sound of a mouth sucking a snow cone; "burp"—the sound of indigestion. Can you write a poem full of onomatopoeia?

Ask your students to identify the rhyming words in each poem. Explain that both poems rely on the use of end rhyme, but that Aldis used end rhyme differently in each poem. In "About Candy," she used couplets, two successive lines that rhyme with one another. Explain that the end-rhyme pattern for the couplets in "About Candy" is *aa, bb, cc, dd.*

In "Crunch and Lick," Aldis used a different end-rhyme pattern that looks like this: *abcb, defef.* Explain to your students that while some of the rhymes in this poem match syllable for syllable, such as "do" and "to," others put together words of different syllables, such as "popsicles" and "trickle," that are nonetheless said to rhyme, though not perfectly.

Distribute large index cards to your students. Have them write the name of one favorite food on each index card.

Divide the class into small groups. Have each group brainstorm rhyming words that describe each food. For example, a group might describe ice cream as neat and sweet or lumpy and bumpy.

Collect the cards, alphabetize them, and file them in a file box. Encourage your students to add new rhymes to the file and to check it for inspiration when they write poetry.

- Choose a rhyme scheme, such as *abab, cdcd;* then use it to write a poem about foods you like. If you wish, you may work with cards from the file. Don't forget to use onomatopoeia.

Bring in simple recipes (such as pudding, fruit salad, or an ice-cream sundae). Copy the recipes on the chalkboard. Work with small groups to write rhyming couplets that describe how to prepare these foods.

Ask your students to bring in candy wrappers and magazine advertisements for food. Your students can then use these items to make a collage. Ask your students to write food poems to accompany their artwork, and paste the poems right on the collages.

CRUNCH AND LICK
by Dorothy Aldis

Popcorn crunches.
Peanuts do.
The cone part of an ice-cream cone
Is wonderful for crunching, too.
Things to lick are candy sticks,
Rainbow-colored popsicles,
Chocolate sauce when it begins
To leak and trickle
Down our chins.

ABOUT CANDY
by Dorothy Aldis

I say to lick a candy stick
Until it's sharp enough to prick.
If you've a lemon drop, then tuck it
Way inside your cheek and suck it.
To bite it would be very wrong
Because it would not last you long.
But the only thing to do
With a caramel is chew.

Poetry

HARLEM HOPSCOTCH

BY MAYA ANGELOU

SOURCE

Meyer, Sister J. Eleanor. "Neighborhoods: Maya Angelou's "Harlem Hopscotch," *English Journal,* v77 n5 September 1988, pp. 86-88.

BRIEF DESCRIPTION

Students participate in class discussion, read a contemporary poem, participate in oral reading, write a rap, and write a poem using the concept of extended metaphor.

OBJECTIVE

To examine contemporary poetry and the extended metaphor.

PROCEDURES

Begin a discussion with your students about success. Discuss actual success and the potential achievement of success. Read the poem by Maya Angelou on page 154 to your students.

HARLEM HOPSCOTCH
by Maya Angelou

One foot down, then hop! It's hot.
Good things for the ones that's got.
Another jump, now to the left.
Everybody for hisself.

In the air, now both feet down.
Since you black, don't stick around.
Food is gone, the rent is due,
Curse and cry and then jump two.

All the people out of work,
Hold for three, then twist and jerk.
Cross the line, they count you out.
That's what hopping's all about.

Both feet flat, the game is done.
They think I lost. I think I won.

Ask for volunteers to read the poem aloud. Ask your students to pretend they are playing hopscotch as they read the poem.

✦ What is the poem about?

✦ Have you ever been to Harlem?

Discuss the concept of the extended metaphor. The poem is about simple childhood play translated into the complex game of life.

✦ Why did Angelou use the words she did?

Lead a discussion about the form of the poem. Point out that it is in the traditional sonnet format, but not in iambic pentameter, though it does have a couplet ending.

Talk about "poetic license" and American Black dialect. Use of words like "hisself" and phrases like "since you black" are acceptable only if you know what you're doing!

✦ Using Angelou's poem, write a rap and present it to the class.

Ask your students to spend ten minutes free-writing on how "Harlem Hopscotch" speaks to them.

✦ Think about a favorite childhood experience. Now, use that experience as an extended metaphor to describe a recent life experience or life itself. Write a poem using this concept.

"A Narrow Fellow in the Grass"

by Emily Dickinson

Source

Marhafer, David J. "Reading a Poem by Dickinson: A Psychological Approach," *English Journal,* v77 n1 January 1988, pp. 59-63.

Brief Description

Students use Freud's theory of the three levels of consciousness to write an interpretation of Emily Dickinson's poem, "A Narrow Fellow in the Grass."

Objective

To write about a topic seriously; to learn to express oneself articulately.

Procedures

As a pre-reading exercise, ask your students to write a paper about their greatest fear. Ask for volunteers to read their papers aloud to the class. Have them read their papers to themselves and bracket the sentence that most clearly identifies the greatest fear. Now, ask the students to write a word, phrase, or sentence that would best describe their fear.

Read Emily Dickinson's "A Narrow Fellow in the Grass," on page 156, aloud to your class.

- Read the poem silently.
- Write a question that is critical to your understanding of the poem. The answer to this question should shed light on the meaning of the poem.

Compile the questions into a list, type them, and give copies of the list to the students for them to consider as they reread the poem.

A Narrow Fellow in the Grass
by Emily Dickinson

A narrow Fellow in the grass
Occasionally rides—
You may have met Him—did you not
His notice sudden is—

The Grass divides as with a comb—
A spotted shaft is seen—
And then it closes at your feet
And opens further on—

He likes a Boggy Acre
A floor too cool for Corn—
Yet when A Boy, and Barefoot—
I more than once at Noon

Have passed, I thought, a Whip lash
Unbraiding in the Sun
When stooping to secure it
It wrinkled and was gone—

Several of Nature's People
I know, and they know me—
I feel for them a transport
Of cordiality—

But never met the Fellow
Attended or alone
Without a tighter breathing
And Zero at the Bone—

Discuss with your class Freud's theory of the three levels of consciousness going on inside our minds. Carl R. Green and William R. Sanford's *Psychology: A Way to Grow* (New York: Amsco, 1983) is useful in clarifying the relationship among the conscious, preconscious, and the unconscious mind. Ask your students to discuss the theory, and keep the discussion going until you collectively arrive at a working definition of the three levels.

Divide your class into three groups. Assign to each group one of the levels of consciousness.

- Read the poem according to your group's assigned level of consciousness.

- Ask one person in your group to act as secretary and write down the thoughts and answers to the questions that the whole class wrote earlier, but now from the point of view of your group's level of consciousness.

- Organize your thoughts and write an interpretation of the poem at your assigned level of consciousness.

Discuss their interpretations with your class. Discuss the questions that will have arisen as the groups formed their interpretations.

- Respond to the following:

It is said of many youthful activities and perceptions that "ignorance is bliss." Think of a time—or times—when you were young and you ate something, or ventured an undertaking, that now in the "wisdom of your years" gives you pause. Perhaps you had experiences that were so terrifying that you have never been willing to undertake them again to this day!

- Write about this situation. Try to articulate so precisely that your fear or distaste becomes palpable to the reader.

Comments

The students' level of honesty and seriousness of purpose improve with this exercise. Readers see each other struggling with meaning. Some students may grow into independent interpreters brave enough to venture an uncertain reading. By using psychological models to enrich their insights, students acquire a language with which to express themselves articulately.

Sharing Poetry with Students
by Eve Merriam and Lilian Moore

Source

de Fina, Allan. "'Poetry Pages' Readers' Workshop," *Instructor,* v101 n2 September 1991, pp. 90-91.

Merriam, Eve. "Sharing Poetry with Children," *Learning,* v14 n2 September 1985, pp. 78-80.

Brief Description

Students participate in class discussion, word webbing, poetry reading, choral reading, and a writing assignment.

Objective

To introduce students to poetry and to explore it on their own terms.

Procedures

Some young people think of poetry as a specialty that you serve up only on red-letter days, like Thanksgiving turkey or Christmas plum pudding. Poetry, however, is part of how we really live our lives and how we truly feel every day.

Before reading any poetry, ask your students the following questions:

1. What is a poem?
2. How do we know one when we see one?
3. Does it have to rhyme?
4. Who writes poetry?
5. What do poets write about?

On the chalkboard, draw an idea map or word web with the word "poem" at the center. As your students respond to each of the questions above, group their ideas into categories with headings such as "poet," "form," "shape," "topic," and "idea."

Read the poem by Lilian Moore, on page 160 to your class:

Moore's desire for her readers is that they enjoy poetry's power of lift to the imagination.

- Who is Lilian Moore talking to?
- What does she mean when she tells you to "hang glide" and "sail?"
- Explain the sense of the poem's ending: "Trust the poem."

Now, begin a new category called "feelings" on your word web. Include ideas about the feelings your students may get from poetry.

Read the poem by Eve Merriam, on page 160, to your class:

In this poem, Merriam compares the pleasure of reading poetry to the pleasure of eating.

- How do you "eat" a poem?
- Imagine eating a juicy piece of fruit. Think about how it feels in your mouth, how it tastes, how it makes you feel.
- Make your own comparisons between reading a poem and eating a piece of fruit. Remember that Merriam points out that there is nothing left "to throw away." (Every word counts.)

Add your students' comparisons and ideas to the word web on the chalkboard.

Read the poems chorally. Divide your class into small groups. Assign each group member a particular line from the poem. Give your students time to rehearse, and then have the groups read their poems to the class.

- Write a poem, essay, or story about one of the ideas generated by the word web.

It would be fun for your students (and for you) if you would take part in this assignment with them by writing a poem, essay, or story. Share your work with the class. Take part with them in the writing process: Read parts to them early in the process; take their editorial suggestions to heart; share the finished written piece with them.

COMMENTS

"In a way, a poem is like a can of frozen juice. When you add three cans of water, you get the prose version."

—Eve Merriam

Go with the Poem
by Lilian Moore

Go with the poem.
Hang glide
above new landscape
into other weather.

Sail the poem.
Lift.
Drift over treetops
and towers.

Loop with the poem.
Swoop, dip.
Land.
Where?
Trust the poem.

How to Eat a Poem
by Eve Merriam

Don't be polite.
Bite in.
Pick it up with your fingers
and lick the juice that may
run down your chin.
It is ready and ripe now,
wherever you are.

You do not need a knife or
fork or spoon
or plate or napkin or
tablecloth.

For there is no core
or stem
or rind
or pit
or seed
or skin
to throw away.

"THE FURY OF OVERSHOES"

BY ANNE SEXTON

SOURCE

Zancanella, Don. "Memory, Power, and Poetry: Sexton's 'Fury of Overshoes,'" *English Journal* v76 n7 November 1987, pp. 84-88.

BRIEF DESCRIPTION

Students read a poem, participate in class discussion, and complete a writing project.

OBJECTIVE

With the help of Anne Sexton's poem, students see that the changes they are going through as they mature are normal.

PROCEDURES

Read the poem by Anne Sexton, on page 163, to your students.

- What is the earliest thing you can recall about yourself as a writer?

Spend time talking about what it was like to begin writing. Remind your students of the fat black pencils and the green penmanship paper with large lines.

- Do you remember feeling angry or helpless because you were too little to do what you wanted?

Give each student a chance to tell his or her own story about being small and helpless.

- First, think about a favorite object from your childhood. Write a short essay about this object as you see it and feel about it now as a student.

- Next, write a short essay about the object as you saw it and felt about it when you were a small child.

- Last, write a short essay about the object as you might see it and feel about it as an adult.

- Read each of your essays.

- What changes have you gone through in your thinking from when you were little to today?

- Are you still "little" in some ways? What ways?

- What changes do you think you will have gone through by the time you reach adulthood?

Comment

Developmental psychologists talk about the transformation that children undergo from self-centeredness to a sense of their place in the world. Part of that change is the ability to look forward and backward through time and see one's past and future "from the outside," as it were. Sexton's poem helps early teens understand that transformation.

THE FURY OF OVERSHOES
by Anne Sexton

They sit in a row
outside the kindergarten,
black, red, brown, all
with those brass buckles.
Remember when you couldn't
buckle your own
shoe
or cut your own meat,
and the tears
running down like mud
because you fell off your
tricycle?
Remember, big fish,
when you couldn't swim
and simply slipped under
like a stone frog?
The world wasn't yours.
It belonged to the big people.
Under your bed
sat the wolf
and he made a shadow
when cars passed by
at night.
They made you give up
your nightlight
and your teddy
and your thumb.
Oh, overshoes,
don't you
remember me,
pushing you up and down
in the winter snow?
Oh thumb,
I want a drink,
it is dark,
where are the big people,
when will I get there,
taking giant steps
all day,
each day
and thinking
nothing of it?

TEACHING LITERATURE BY WOMEN AUTHORS

COLONIAL POETRY
BY ANNE BRADSTREET

SOURCE

Sanders, Beverly. *Women in American History: A Series. Book One, Women in the Colonial Era and The Early American Republic 1607-1820*. American Federation of Teachers, Washington, D.C. 1979. 58pp. **ED 186 340**

BRIEF DESCRIPTION

Students think about the life of a famous colonial poet, read her poetry, research her life and times, write an essay, and complete a group research project.

OBJECTIVES

Students read poetry from an historical perspective, correlating the poet's life with her poetry.

PROCEDURES

Anne Bradstreet (1612-1672) lived in the Massachusetts Bay Colony in pre-Revolutionary America. She became the colony's foremost poet. Her husband, Simon Bradstreet, and her father, Thomas Dudley, were men of great eminence in the colony's affairs (her father was its governor for a time). Anne Bradstreet was in no way a social outsider; in England, where she had spent the first eighteen years of her life, she had been born and raised a gentlewoman. In England, she received a thorough education, becoming well-acquainted with the Bible and with the literature of her time. Privileged status, however, did not shield her from the sufferings of the women of her generation. This is reflected in her volume of poems, *The Tenth Muse Lately Sprung Up in America*, which was published in England in 1650 without Bradstreet's knowledge.

The poet tells of her frequent illnesses, the burning of her house, the births of her eight children, the deaths of her grandchildren, and her tender love for her husband.

+ Read the poem by Anne Bradstreet. As you are reading, look for clues about life for a woman in colonial America.

- Write an essay on Anne Bradstreet. Answer the following questions as you write. Use Anne Bradstreet's poetry and the history of her time as your resources for factual information.

1. What part did women play in the permanent settlement of English North America?
2. What advantages were offered to attract Englishwomen to the colonies?
3. What was life like for a colonial woman?
4. How did the life of a woman of privilege differ from that of a woman of poorer means?
5. Why was Anne's poetry looked on as "rebellious" or out-of-character for a woman in colonial America?

Divide your class into groups, and ask each group to do the following:

- Colonial women usually excelled in needlework, and many of the products of their skill—samplers, quilts, embroidery, needlepoint—are on display in museums and historical societies. Beautifully illustrated books devoted to these now valuable antiques are available. Do research on at least one kind of needlework practiced by colonial women, and prepare a class exhibit.

TO MY DEAR AND LOVING HUSBAND
by Anne Bradstreet

If ever two were one, then surely we.
If ever man were lov'd by wife, then thee;
If ever wife was happy in a man,
Compare with me, ye women, if you can,
I prize thy love more than whole Mines of gold,
Or all the riches that the East doth hold.
My love is such that Rivers cannot quench,
Nor ought but love from thee, give recompence.
Thy love is such I can no way repay,
The heavens reward thee manifold I pray.
Then while we live, in love lets so persever,
That when we live no more, we may live ever.

"AN ORDINARY WOMAN"
BY LUCILLE CLIFTON

SOURCE

Reed, Beth, ed., and others. *Toward a Feminist Transformation of the Academy: II. Proceedings of the Annual GLCA Women's Studies Conference.* 1980. 92pp. **ED 251 400**

BRIEF DESCRIPTION

Students keep a journal of their feelings as they read selected poems, participate in discussions, and write an essay.

OBJECTIVE

Students get a woman's perspective in Black literature.

PROCEDURES

In her poetry, Lucille Clifton gives us a woman's perspective in Black literature. Instead of juggling, slighting, or submerging concerns of gender for those of race, or vice versa, she gives us a dual vision, a double perspective. Clifton writes of herself as a Black woman—one who is trying to find herself as both female and of African descent.

As your students study the poems of Lucille Clifton, ask them to keep a journal of their ideas about the poems they are reading—comments, reactions, confusions—anything they care to write.

As your students read the poem by Clifton on page 169, ask them to make notes on how the poet sees herself.

How does this portrait differ from traditional Black matriarchal portraits?

Note: Students may not understand the term "Black matriarch." A useful book for your students to read is *The Autobiography of Miss Jane Pitman* by Ernest Gaines. This book is also available on video cassette. To get a different perspective of a Black matriarch, you may want to use *Gone with the Wind* by Margaret Mitchell, which is also available on video cassette.

- How are Black matriarchs portrayed on television?

- How are Black matriarchs portrayed in advertising?
- How are Black matriarchs portrayed in other books that you have read?

A second characteristic of Lucille Clifton's poetry is the honest way that she deals with relationships among women—the community of women. Ask your students to read the poem, on page 170, about Clifton's relationship with her four daughters.

- What images does Clifton use to describe her daughters?
- Why do you think she used these images?

The other poem by Clifton that shows the relationships among women, on page 171, is written in Black dialect.

- What has happened to the two "sisters" in this poem?
- Why did they grease their black, ashy legs and touch up the curly edges of their hair?
- What are some differences between growing up as a White female and growing up as a Black female?
- Using different colored pens or pencils, mark the mood changes in the poem.
- Do you think the women finally became accepting of the fact that they are Black females? If so, how long did it take?
- From your journal entries about the three poems, write an essay about the poetry of Lucille Clifton. Answer the following questions as you write:
  - Did you like Clifton's poetry?
  - What of herself as a person does Lucille Clifton show in her poems?
  - Are there any issues/elements that seem to be present in all three of these poems?
  - Do you feel sympathy with any of Clifton's personal interests?
  - Do you feel differently about life from the way that Clifton does?
  - Does her poetry give you a different perspective on being a Black woman?

An Ordinary Woman
by Lucille Clifton

the thirty eighth year
of my life,
plain as bread
round as a cake
an ordinary woman.

i had expected to be
smaller than this,
more beautiful,
wiser in Afrikan ways,
more confident,
i had expected
more than this.

i will be forty soon.
my mother once was forty.

my mother died at forty four,
a woman of sad countenance
leaving behind a girl
awkward as a stork.
my mother was thick,
her hair was a jungle and
she was very wise
and beautiful
and sad.

i have dreamed dreams
for you mama
more than once.
i have wrapped me
in your skin
and made you live again
more than once.
i have taken the bones you
hardened
and built daughters
and they blossom and
promise fruit
like Afrikan trees.
i am a woman now.
an ordinary woman.

in the thirty eighth
year of my life,
surrounded by life,
a perfect picture of
blackness blessed,
i had not expected this
loneliness.

if it is western,
if it is the final
if in the middle of my life
i am turning the final turn
into the shining dark
let me come to it whole
and holy
not afraid
not lonely
out of my mother's life
into my own.
into my own.

i had expected more than
this.
i had not expected to be
an ordinary woman.

LAST NOTE TO MY GIRLS
For Sid, Ricca, Gilly and Neen
by Lucille Clifton

my girls
my girls
my almost me
mellowed in a brown bag
held tight and straining
at the top
like a good lunch
until the bag turned weak and wet
and burst in our honeymoon rooms.
we wiped the mess and
dressed you in our name and
here you are
my girls
my girls
forty quick fingers
reaching for the door.

i command you to be
good runners
to go with grace
go well in the dark and
make for high ground
my dearest girls
my girls
my more than me.

SISTERS
by Lucille Clifton

me and you be sisters.
we be the same.
me and you
coming from the same place.
me and you
be greasing our legs
touching up our edges.
me and you
be scared of rats
be stepping on roaches.
me and you
come running high down purdy street one time
and mama laugh and shake her head at
me and you.
me and you
got babies
got black
let our hair go back
be loving ourselves
be loving ourselves
be sisters.
only where you sing
i poet.

THE MEANING OF HER POEMS
BY JULIA MALOTT

SOURCE

Northern Kentucky University ReEntry Center, 1980-1990. 10 Year Anniversary Celebration. 1990. 46 pp. **ED 344 026**

BRIEF DESCRIPTION

Students answer a series of questions, read a series of poems, make lists, and participate in class discussion.

OBJECTIVES

Students gain a better understanding of poetry; they use this understanding to discover the meaning partially hidden behind one woman's poetic words.

PROCEDURES

The following poems by Julia Malott were taken from a collection of poems by individuals who have either been through the program offered by the ReEntry Center at Northern Kentucky University or have otherwise had their lives touched and changed by the Center's existence. After a general discussion of the meaning of poetry, your students will read a series of poems by one author, examine each poem, and determine what the poems are about.

Ask your students as a group to discuss the following questions:

+ What is poetry?
+ How does poetry differ from other writing?
+ What is unique in the language of poetry?
+ What makes a good poem?

Ask your students to read the poems by Julia Malott, beginning on page 174.

Propose the following questions to your class as a whole:

1. What do we know already about this poem?

    + Using all four poems, make a list of *known* items that the poems tell you.

2. What do we want to find out?

    ✦ Now make a list of *unknown* items or questions that you have about the poems.

Act as scribe and ask your students to give you their lists as you write the lists on the chalkboard.

3. How will we go about finding out?

    ✦ What can we do to find out the answers to our questions?

4. How will we show what we have found out?

    ✦ How can we present our findings?

Read the following brief biography of Julia Malott to your students to help with their findings:

Julia Malott's poetry is a valuable contribution to a collection of women's writings by the Northern Kentucky University ReEntry Center. She is a person who has achieved many of her personal and professional goals.

Malott entered Northern Kentucky University through the ReEntry Center Program in 1982, at age 20 and as a single parent with a 17-month-old daughter, Ashley. Five years later, Malott graduated from the University with a 3.5 grade-point average with a major in Philosophy. She attended graduate school at the State University of New York at Stony Brook and completed her master's degree. She has completed her course work for her doctoral degree and plans to write her dissertation.

While at NKU, Malott received several awards for her poetry, including the Outstanding Freshman Writing Award and the Creative Writing Award; her poetry was also featured in the NKU *Alumni Magazine*. She also placed fourth in a national poetry contest.

Julia Malott believes that warmth, sensitivity, and strength are at the heart of all women. She has said that through education and her travels on her own personal journey, she has learned that she is much more than a face that can smile. She has accepted the challenges of many life transitions, and her poetry provides a voice for women who seek to find their sense of self.

POSTURES
by Julia Malott

i.
Your forehead fits neatly into your rounded hands,
your feet spread and firmly set, flatly,
on the floor beneath you.
You do not move but breathe in
quiet gasps, comprehending.
If I shift toward you,
you stiffen and flee and do not move
so I keep my touch though my fingers sing
in hoarse circling cries above you.

ii.
I sit, feet propped, temple to palm, elbow to knee
watching the black space to my right which reddens,
burns, breaks into blue.
White light flames across the sky.
It is morning in the air; it is morning on the ground
where you turn in your sleep, long body, dark eyes
dancing a sleeper's rhythm, as I hurl, jetspeed, away.

THE LAB
by Julia Malott

She lies pinned, exposed,
the frog at stake,
a neat dissection before him.
Sift, analyze, question—
he works slowly,
guided by concrete presuppositions.
Examination finished,
he cleans his scalpel with careful pride.
Subjective annoyances
are tossed, by a swift hand, over the shoulder.
He makes no wish.

Toy Box
by Julia Malott

I can't believe your eyes faded
From crystal blue
To a dull grey
Overnight.
I guess with the changing light,
My childish dreams
Were tucked away
Into my toy box
With the threadbare promises
And broken playthings
That collected dust
And lost their stuffing
While my eyes were closed.

Sisters
by Julia Malott

Those who at birth
found a fertile field in which to play
know nothing of we who were born
throat-deep in sewage
where each breath is roulette
and each word drills echoes
into empty vessels
reserved for love.

She cried all night once,
clutching her dead cat to her breast,
rocking, humming, while blood dried
between her fingers and the long curls of fur
offered no warmth.
She found a page once, scarred by my words,
and grabbed, frightened, for someone not there.
She knew how easily I could leave.

We share the same longing,
trapped as we are under the same glass, scorching.
Our shared vessel in silent screams deafens.

"Our Root Cellar"

by Lois Prante Stevens

Source

Thompson, Lowell, and Sheldon Schmidt. *North Dakota Teachers' Center. Second Special Edition.* Center for Teaching and Learning, Grand Forks, North Dakota. October 1989. 29 pp. **ED 317 466**

Brief Description

Students read a poem, write an adventure story, participate in oral reading, complete a handout, and answer questions.

Objective

Students come to understand more about the turn-of-the-century farm family's surroundings: their buildings, tools, work, equipment, food, and machines.

Procedures

Let your students find out what a "root cellar" is as they carry out the activities in this lesson.

Ask your students to read the poem by Lois Prante Stevens on page 177.

Our Root Cellar
by Lois Prante Stevens

Mama tugged the heavy trap door up
And pushed it to one side on the kitchen floor,
Revealing the black hole.
She said I must climb down into the cellar
And bring her things she needed for supper.
I dared not say no,
But I would rather have taken a "licking"
Than descend into that dank, fetid space
That stank of garden vegetables stored too long
And goodness knew what else.
Cautiously I backed down the wooden steps,
One hand clinging to the floor.
Mama held the lamp.
Its feeble glow did nothing to dispel my fright.
"Hurry, now," Mama said, "Bring potatoes
And some turnips, too."
I groped toward the potato pile,
Brushing cobwebs from my face,
Bumping a cabbage head hung upside down
From a floor joint.
I could feel the texture of the turnips,
Smooth and round.
I scrambled back toward the shaft of light
And handed up the pan.
Then Mama said, "Bring a jar of plum sauce."
Dismayed, I went back only to find
I'd chosen gooseberries.
Almost frantic now, sure the "boogy-man"
Would get me before I could escape,
I scuttled back, found the right sauce
And scurried up the steps.
Mama pulled the trap door back in place,
Snugged it tight into the floor.
A warm, lighted kitchen, the tea kettle singing,
And Mama's soft, "Now help me peel the potatoes,"
Quelled my quivers of fear.
And I knew I had earned a reprieve.
Tomorrow it would be my sister's turn
To dare those dungeon depths.

Read the following paragraph to your students:

The farm house that Lois lived in did not have a basement. There was, however, a deep hole dug under the floor of the kitchen. A heavy trap door, cut into the wooden floor of the kitchen, could be pulled open to permit someone to back down the wooden steps into the hole. Lois hated it when her mother asked her to go down into the hole because there were cobwebs that she could not see, and the light was, at best, in her words, "a feeble glow."

- Write your own story about Lois's adventure in the "mysterious" hole under the kitchen floor. Answer the following questions as you write your story:

    1. Was it just a hole or was there a tunnel also?
    2. What did Lois find?
    3. Who or what did she meet?
    4. Was she in danger?
    5. Did she get lost?
    6. How did she feel?
    7. Did she meet someone who was friendly to her?
    8. Does she ever get out of the hole?
    9. What was the mystery?
    10. Did she bring anything back with her?

"Publish" your students' stories by hanging them on the walls around the room and let them read one another's writings. Discuss the similarities and differences. Did anyone base their story on a story that they had already read, i.e., *Alice in Wonderland*?

- Are there special places in your home, yard, neighborhood, or school that might encourage you to write another good story? Make a list of "mysterious" places that you know.

Give your students the following handout to complete. This will introduce them to some of the farm supplies, materials, tools, and buildings, the names of which may be unfamiliar to people unacquainted with farm life. Students will be able to determine the use of each.

Poetry

ARE YOU FARM LITERATE?

Match each name in the *Place Name* list with one item in the *What You'll Find There* list.

Place Name	What You'll Find There
1. storm cellar	a. sausage and hams
2. milking parlor	b. maize
3. well house	c. someone afraid, but safe
4. smokehouse	d. a half-moon on the door
5. outhouse	e. cooling pails of milk
6. root cellar	f. a cud chewer
7. corn crib	g. carrots and turnips

Number Correct: _____

Brainstorm and list as many farm buildings as you can. How are they used?

FARM I.Q.

Determine your farm I.Q. by circling the best definition or each of the following terms:

1. Pitch fork
    a) a fork-ball pitcher
    b) used to pitch forks instead of horseshoes
    c) used to pitch cut grass and hay

2. Horse mower
    a) gives horses haircuts
    b) mows tall grass
    c) mows tall horses' long tails

3. Potato ricer
    a) makes mashed potatoes look like rice
    b) cuts potatoes up into seed-potatoes
    c) another name for an Idaho potato

4. Threshing machine
    a) automatically spanks naughty farm boys and girls
    b) shoos away flies
    c) removes seeds from heads of grain

5. Carpet beater
    a) used to beat down hay to make a soft carpet for sleeping cows and horses
    b) used to beat dust from rugs and carpets
    c) used to beat eggs flat like a carpet to make scrambled eggs and crêpes

Number correct _____

Brainstorm and list as many additional farming tools as you can. How are they used?

Read the following paragraph to your students:

A root cellar needed to be both cool and dry to keep roots, bulbs, tubers (potatoes, etc.), and vegetables edible during the fall and winter months of the year. Other vegetables were canned and stored in jars in the root cellar. The roots stored whole and fresh included carrots, turnips, parsnips, beets, sugar beets, radishes, and rutabagas (also called Swedish turnips or the "baggy root"). Root cellars, whether under the house or dug into a bank somewhere else in the ground, frequently doubled as a storm cellar for protection from tornadoes.

- List the words Lois used to describe the root cellar.
- How did she feel about the root cellar?
- List the words you used in your adventure story.
- What were your feelings in your story?

Answers to "Are You Farm Literate?": 1-c; 2-f; 3-e; 4-a; 5-d; 6-g; 7-b

Answers to "Farm I.Q.": 1-c; 2-b; 3-a; 4-c; 5-b

"The Peddler"

by Lois Prante Stevens

Source

Thompson, Lowell, and Sheldon Schmidt. *North Dakota Teachers' Center. Second Special Edition*. Center for Teaching and Learning, Grand Forks, North Dakota. October 1989. 29 pp. **ED 317 466**

Brief Description

Students participate in group discussion, read a poem, complete a list, watch a movie.

Objective

Students understand the meaning of the term "peddler."

Procedures

Ask your students to share their thoughts about the following questions:

1. How do you gain a first impression of someone you meet? What is the very first thing you notice? What details do you pick up on to build your impression?

2. What tells you that you might like the person or might not like the person?

3. What should you know about a person before you decide what kind of a person he or she is?

4. Does it make a difference whether the person you have just met is your age? A teenager? An adult? An old person?

5. Sometimes we give names to people because they dress differently from the way we do or talk differently. How do you think the label affects the person labeled?

Read the following information to your students:

SELLING DOOR-TO-DOOR

All across our state, people sell products door-to-door. They walk up one side of a street and knock at every door; then they cross to the other side of the street and walk down that side and knock at every door.

Sometimes they drive through the countryside stopping at the farm homes. In 1918 these people were called peddlers.

Lois Prante was a peddler when, as a young child, she tried to sell her packages of seeds to rural neighbors. Peddlers are children selling seeds, candy, or tickets for school raffles. Peddlers are college students at their summer jobs selling books to children, or pots and pans to homemakers. The Schwan truck person, the Avon salesperson, the encyclopedia seller, the Fuller brush person, the Amway person, and the Shaklee person are all peddlers. A church missionary who knocks on your door could be called a peddler; missionaries peddle religious ideas door-to-door, and some do have religious materials for sale. An insurance salesperson could be a peddler if he or she is the kind who just comes to your door without an appointment. So is a magazine seller; a vacuum cleaner salesperson; a person selling greeting cards, thank-you cards, birthday cards, and get-well-soon and holiday cards. These are all peddlers, and so are Girl Scouts selling cookies.

The definition of a peddler is "one who travels about selling." When Lois Prante was a young girl living on a farm, the various peddlers were always welcome. They sold specialty items that were sometimes of higher quality than the items in the village store. Buying from the peddler was convenient; the peddler came right to the farm-house door so the shopper did not have to waste time making a trip to town. Nowadays, the peddlers are on the TV shopping channels, or they mail their catalogues directly to our mailboxes.

Ask your students to share the thoughts and feelings that are stirred by the following questions:

1. How do you feel when a stranger comes to your door?

2. Do you feel differently if the stranger is a young person like yourself or an older person? Should you feel different?

3. What should you expect a door-to-door salesperson or a stranger to do before they ask for admittance to your home?

4. Should school groups, church groups, and other community groups let parents and/or the whole community know when there is going to be a fund drive, or the sale of tickets for a raffle?

5. What have you been told to do when a stranger comes to your door and you are home alone; when the telephone rings and you are pretty sure it is not someone you know calling; if a parent is late getting home?

6. Does it help you to feel secure when you know the rules and when you know that you are following those rules? Talk about following the rules, and share your experiences.

Either read the poem by Lois Prante, on page 186, to your students, or have them read it on their own. Ask them to note the excitement that Lois felt about the coming of the peddler.

Ask your students to note how Mother feels about the peddler's coming. What emotions are going through Mother's mind?

Children in Lois's time rarely got new dresses and presents. They had only a few toys, and treats were usually homemade.

1. When do you feel really excited about getting something new?

2. Do you usually get to buy some new toy each time you go shopping with your parents at Wal-Mart, Target, K-Mart, or one of the toy stores?

3. Should you always expect to get something new? How does a child know when he or she is spoiled or is being spoiled? Do you have to get lots of new things to be happy?

4. Do you know any children your age who don't care whether they get anything new all summer long? How about children who love to play baseball and who are on a baseball team and play with the same old bat, same old ball, and same old glove all summer?

5. What do you have to play with that usually keeps you occupied and satisfied for long periods of time?

6. If you get a sweet treat every day, is it really a treat or are you just being given junk food? How do you decide? Do you usually eat at least one meal a day that includes all four food groups? Do you think it is important to do so? Why or why not?

Salespeople that fit under the category "peddler" are still common today. A partial list includes the following:

- Avon ladies
- Schwan truck drivers
- Mary Kay cosmetic experts
- Tupperware representatives
- the folks from Amway
- Shaklee dealers
- Kirby vacuum cleaner agents
- hosts on the TV sales channels

- Ask your parents to help you do the following with this list:
    1. Put a check mark next to any of the persons on the list who have come to your door.
    2. Have your parents help you to think of other people who come to the door to sell things. Add them to the list.
    3. Have your parents help you list (next to the peddler's name) what the family typically buys from each of the persons who come to the door.
- Bring your list to school to share what you have learned about the peddlers in your community and what they usually sell to your family.

There are movies/videos that have rather famous peddlers in them. The most famous would probably be the band-instrument salesman in *The Music Man.* You might have a sleepover in your classroom, watch the movie, and play games. Or, you might join forces with the instrumental music teacher and take a couple of hours in the afternoon to watch the video.

- Think back to the list of peddlers you examined with your parents. Are all peddlers swindlers? Or, do they sell door-to-door, like people in stores, in an honest effort to earn a living?

The Peddler
by Lois Prante

Our Mama saw the scraggly horse and cart
Drive right into the barnyard from the road.
She thought it was the Watkins' man and sent
My sister out to ask him for whole cloves
And lemon flavoring and ginger spice.
But when he swung around and spread apart
The doors across the back, there were no shelves
With spice filled tins, but rolls of lace and tiers
Of brightly colored thread. The ribbons made
A rainbow right before my sister's eyes.
She gaped and ran for Mama, shouting, "Come!
Come quick, 'cause it's the peddler, with his store
On wheels," and Mama wrapped a shawl around
Her shoulders and came out to look. She chose
Some needles and red ribbons for our hair,
And then the peddler said, "I've goods in bolts.
Fine satins, moire silk and all-wool, too."
Then from his pile he pulled a bolt of silk
With woven Roman Stripes in orange and blue
And green and yellow...interspaced with black.
He saw my sister's yearning eyes, "Just right
To make a girlie's skirt," and Bernice pled
With her, but Mama said it was too dear
And tugged a bolt of deep blue wool out from
Beneath the rest and fingered it and found
It soft and light, and chose plaid ribbon she
Would use as piping for the collar trim.
He brought the bolt into the house and spread
The cloth out on our dining table top.
Then Mama said to bring the match box from
The warming oven on the stove and took
Her shears and snipped a thread off from the end.
She held a match to it and watched it curl
And roll into a crusty ball of ash
That told her it was wool—not cotton packed.
She measured out the length she'd need to make
Two dresses for her girls, and talked him down
A bit from his first price. When he was gone
She smiled at the good bargain she had made.
At Christmastime we wore our dresses when
We went to visit Grandpa—on the train.
Our Grandpa romped with us and let us brush
His thick white hair and listened to us speak
Out all the "pieces" we had learned by heart.

Poetry

REVOLUTIONARY WAR ERA POETRY
BY PHILLIS WHEATLEY

SOURCE

Sanders, Beverly. *Women in American History: A Series. Book One, Women in the Colonial Era and The Early American Republic 1607-1820.* American Federation of Teachers, Washington, D.C. 1979. 58pp. **ED 186 340**

BRIEF DESCRIPTION

Students think about the life of a famous revolutionary-war era poet, read her poetry, research her life and times, write an essay, and complete a presentation.

OBJECTIVES

Students read poetry in an historical perspective to see how the poet lived during her time and how her historical context informed her poetry.

PROCEDURES

Read the following short biography of Phillis Wheatley to your students:

During the Revolutionary War, Black Americans played significant parts. A Black woman who achieved fame in the period of the Revolution was Phillis Wheatley (c. 1753-1784). Probably born in Africa, Wheatley was bought in 1761 directly from a slave ship by a wealthy Boston merchant, John Wheatley. As it was the custom at that time for slaves to take the last name of their owner, she became Phillis Wheatley.

Perhaps because of her unusual intelligence and gentle manners, she was brought up as a pampered child of the family rather than as a slave, and she was educated by the older children of the family. By the time she was in her teens, Phillis Wheatley was learning Latin, reading English literature, and beginning to write poetry. She became something of a curiosity among influential friends of the Wheatley family. Although her poetry was not outstanding, it was considered to be an amazing accomplishment at a time when few Black people had any opportunities for education and when most were regarded by Whites as inferior to themselves in mental ability.

In 1773, Phillis Wheatley went to England, where she was a great success among the aristocrats and where a book of her verse was published entitled *Poems on Various Subjects, Religious and Moral*. After she returned to America, Phyllis's rather sheltered life changed due to the breakup of the Wheatley family circle and the coming of the Revolution. The public had lost interest in her, though there was a brief flurry of interest when her patriotic poem, "His Excellency General Washington," was published in April 1776, and she visited the General at his headquarters in Cambridge. She had her freedom, but she couldn't earn her living writing poetry.

Phyllis married a free Black man named John Peters, who—though he seems to have been a person of some education—failed to support her and the three children she bore him. Her fragile health broke under the strain of poverty and the deaths of two of her children. She was finally reduced to working as a domestic in a boarding house to support herself and her remaining child. They both died on the same day in December 1784, when Phyllis was less than 30 years old.

Ask your students to read the poem by Phyllis Wheatley on pages 189-190.

- How did Phillis Wheatley's life differ from the lives of other slaves during the Revolutionary War era?

- Phillis Wheatley's poems were written for special occasions.
  They are filled with the classical references then admired as appropriate decoration in formal verse. Occasionally, she reminds the reader of the tragedy of slavery, and she voices her love of freedom. How does this poem express the hopes that the American Revolution brought to Black men and women?

- Write an essay on Phillis Wheatley. Use Phillis Wheatley's poetry and the history of her time as your resources of factual information.

- Combine her poems and biography into a presentation on this famous woman. The presentation can take any format you wish—bulletin board, booklet, poster, newspaper, commercial. Get the format approved by your teacher ahead of time.

TO THE RIGHT HON. WILLIAM EARL OF DARTMOUTH, HIS MAJESTY'S SECRETARY OF STATE FOR NORTH AMERICA
by Phillis Wheatly

Hail! happy day! when Smiling like the Morn,
Fair Freedom rose, New England to adorn.
The northern clime, beneath her genial ray,
Beholds exulting, thy Paternal Sway,
For big with hope, her race no longer mourns,
Each Soul expands, each ardent bosom burns,
While in thy hand, with pleasure, we behold
The Silken reins, and Freedom's charms unfold!
Long lost to Realms beneath the northern Skies,
She Shines supreme, while hated Faction dies,
Soon as he Saw the triumph long desir'd
Thus from the Splendors of the rising Sun.
The Sickning Owl explores the dark unknown.
No more of grievance unredress'd complain;
Or injur'd Rights, or groan beneath the chain,
Which Wanton Tyranny with lawless hand,
Made to enslave, O Liberty! thy Land.
My Soul rekindles at thy glorious name
Thy beams essential to the vital Flame.

The Patriot's breast, what Heav'nly virtue warms!
And adds new lustre to his mental charms;
While in thy Speech, the Graces all combine;
Apollos too, with Sons of Thunder Join
Then Shall the Race of injur'd Freedom bless
The Sire, the friend, the messenger of Peace.
While you, my Lord, read o'er th' advent'rous Song
And wonder whence Such daring boldness Sprung:
Hence, flow my wishes for the common good
By feeling hearts alone, best understood.
From Native clime, when Seeming cruel fate
Me snatch'd from Afric's fancy'd happy Seat
Impetuous.—Ah! what bitter pangs molest
What Sorrows labour'd in the Parent breast!
That more than Stone, ne'er Soft compassion mov'd
Who from its Father Seiz'd his much belov'd
Such once my case.—Thus I deplore the day
When Britons weep beneath Tyrannic sway.
To thee, our thanks for favours past are due,
To thee, we still Solicite for the new;

Since in thy pow'r as in thy Will before,
To Sooth the griefs which thou didst then deplore.
May heav'nly grace, the Sacred Sanction give
To all thy works, and thou for ever live,
Not only on the wing of fleeting Fame,
(Immortal Honours grace the Patriot's name!)
Thee to conduct to Heav'ns refulgent fane;
May fiery coursers sweep th' ethereal plain!
Thou, like the Prophet, find the bright abode
Where dwells thy Sire, the Everlasting God.

Annotated Bibliography of Related Resources in the ERIC Database

Citations in this bibliography point to additional ideas for teaching literature by women authors to students in the English/language-arts classroom. The ED numbers for sources in *Resources in Education* are included to enable you to go directly to microfiche collections, or to order materials from the ERIC Document Reproduction Service (EDRS). Contact ERIC Document Reproduction Service (EDRS), 3900 Wheeler Avenue, Alexandria, Virginia 22304; (703) 823-0500 or (800) 227-3742, to order or to obtain current prices of paper copies or microfiche of documents available through EDRS.

Aiken, Susan Hardy. "Women and the Question of Canonicity," *College English,* v48 n3 p288-301 Mar 1986.

> Tells how the traditional Anglo-American literary canon has historically functioned as a paternal edifice, erected on a "plot" that has maintained itself either by keeping women "out" or by keeping them in secondary and dependent positions. Considers revision of the canon as a solution.

Allen, Barbara; and others. *Decision Making Activities for the Grade 9 English Curriculum.* Wappingers Central School District 1, Wappingers Falls, N.Y. 1982. 23 p. [ED 232 147]

> In order to incorporate the elements of personal decision making directly into a ninth-grade English curriculum, the decision-making lessons presented in this paper were written for literature commonly taught in junior-high schools. The paper suggests activities for the following works: *Romeo and Juliet, Flowers for Algernon, The Martian Chronicles, Bless the Beasts and the Children, Anne Frank: The Diary of a Young Girl,* and *The Miracle Worker.* While there is some variety among the lessons presented, most involve writing assignments that are consistent with a ninth-grade writing program.

America's Women of Color: Integrating Cultural Diversity into Non-Sex-Biased Curricula. Secondary Curriculum Guide. 1982. 140 p. [ED 221 501]

> This curriculum guide, designed by secondary-school teachers from the Minnesota school districts of Roseville and St. Paul, helps students to understand the status, needs, and contributions of minority-group women: American Indians, Asian Americans, African Americans, and Hispanics. The guide is intended for use by secondary teachers to integrate relevant aspects of the history, culture, and contributions of minority-group women into existing classroom curricula. Lessons in this curriculum guide are divided according to key concepts: similarities and differences among people, stereotyping, and discrimination. Each lesson plan is structured to emphasize one or more of the key concepts. Subject

area, grade level, and names of teachers who developed the lessons are listed. The minority female group taught about in the lesson is indicated, and major ideas and organizational themes are provided. A summary of each lesson provides teachers with a statement of the content emphasis. Specific behavioral objectives are listed along with teaching procedures and activities designed to help students achieve the objectives. This section on teaching procedures and activities provides discussion questions, worksheets, and ideas. To evaluate the effectiveness of these activities, wrap-up activities are provided in the "Evaluation Procedures" section. A listing of books, articles, and other materials needed for each lesson is included in the resource section following each lesson plan.

Bay, Lois Marie Zinke. *Astute Activities: Increasing Cognitive and Creative Development in the Language Arts Classroom.* 1985. 138 p. [ED 295 156]

Using Mark Twain's *Huckleberry Finn,* John Knowles' *A Separate Peace,* and Maya Angelou's *I Know Why the Caged Bird Sings,* a study examined the effects of astute activities—teaching techniques that increase students' cognitive ability and creativity—on student performance in two senior English classes in a small rural high school. Subjects, nine students from the 1984 senior class and five students from the 1985 senior class, participated in the activities as part of their English class assignments. Activities included mind mapping, brainstorming, creative writing exercises using characters from the novels, and discussions of various issues from the characters' perspectives. Cognitive ability was measured using the Language Arts Test of Cognitive Functioning (LATCF), and writing ability was evaluated with a writing pre- and post-test. Results indicated that astute activities stimulated most students' thinking; increased their awareness of issues; increased the creativity in their work, both written and spoken; and matured their writing. However, LATCF scores showed only slight improvement in overall cognitive functioning for both groups, and pre-test and post-test scores also indicated only slight improvement in writing ability. Implications for improving rural education are addressed. (An appendix includes the LATCF as revised for seniors, pictures of student projects, sample student papers, and student evaluations. Thirty-three references are attached.)

Bender, Patricia A.; Gerber, Nancy F. "Using 'Love Medicine' in the English 102 Classroom: A Study Guide and Resource Manual." Paper presented at the Annual Meeting of the Conference on College Composition and Communication, 1990. 1990. 8 p. [ED 320 162]

This teaching guide offers lesson plans and student assignments based on Louise Erdrich's novel, *Love Medicine,* a celebration of

Chippewa culture that raises an abundance of literary and artistic issues and which also poses numerous sociological and political questions. Included are an introduction to the work, a glossary of literary terms, a biography of the author, an analysis of the novel's structure and theme, suggested questions and topics for writing and discussion, and a conclusion. A section entitled "Using Poetry with the Novel" employs Erdrich's poem "Jacklight" to highlight themes found in *Love Medicine*.

Bischoff, Joan. "Fellow Rebels: Annie Dillard and Maxine Hong Kingston (Reclaiming the Canon)," *English Journal*, v78 n8 p62-67 Dec 1989.

Discusses a pair of books (Annie Dillard's *An American Childhood* and Maxine Hong Kingston's *The Woman Warrior: Memoirs of a Girlhood among Ghosts*) that are well-written, discussion-worthy, and sufficiently alike in content that they can be taught in tandem for comparative purposes as part of a contemporary-literature unit.

Bogert, Edna. "Censorship and 'The Lottery,'" *English Journal*, v74 n1 p45-47 Jan 1985.

Examines Shirley Jackson's short story "The Lottery," written against the background of the Holocaust. Suggests that its theme of mindless and unchallenged tradition, and its corollary theme of control, are meant as a warning that traditions ought to be examined from time to time.

Britton, Eleanore M. "An Approach to 'The Jilting of Granny Weatherall,'" *English Journal*, v76 n4 p35-39 Apr 1987.

Presents an interpretation of Katherine Anne Porter's short story "An Approach to Granny Weatherall" with explanatory material to help students and teachers appreciate and understand it. Notes that this interpretation is contrary to the Roman Catholic theology of sin and punishment on which the story is based.

Byers, Prudence P. "Manipulating Language: A Strategy for Teaching Literature." 1982. 9 p. [ED 225 179]

Literary artists manipulate language. If educators could develop in their students the same sense that language is manipulable, they could help them to appreciate literature better. Emily Dickinson's poem, "I Like to See It Lap the Miles," could be approached by changing it on several levels—graphics, phonics, syntax, and semantics—and seeing how each of these manipulations affects the meaning of the poem. Although this technique does not produce any sort of scientific proof, it does help students see that language can be manipulated and that successful manipulation is not easy. (Three versions of the poem are included.)

Byrne, Mary Ellen. "Flannery O'Connor's Moments of Grace," *Teaching English in the Two Year College,* v15 n4 p250-54 Dec 1988.

   Suggests that instructors of introductory literature courses can teach students how to analyze content and meaning through a pervading theme. Proposes using three of Flannery O'Connor's works, focusing on the "moment of grace" theme in each story, and discussing its central importance in the works.

Byrne, Mary Ellen. "Welty's 'A Worn Path' and Walker's 'Everyday Use': Companion Pieces," *Teaching English in the Two-Year College,* v16 n2 p129-33 May 1989.

   Examines two short stories by women writers—one Black and one White—that celebrate similar values and highlight Black women in family roles yet reveal differences in the authors' perspectives.

Carlson, Margaret. "Teaching Books by and about Women." 1987. 5 p. [ED 281 205]

   Because more than half of all students are female, and because role models are important in forming ideas and images, new attention should be devoted to finding books with heroic, tragic, or significant female characters. Good literature by women can be found in an increasing number of anthologies of women's literature that are now being produced. When teaching women's literature, teachers need to consider their own reactions and those of their students to the differences between men's and women's writing. Women's writing has often been about domestic situations and/or family relationships. Literature by women has often been in the unfamiliar form of journals, diaries, and letters. Also, some women's writing differs in tone by emphasizing more minute details or more intimate emotions than is usual in some men's literature. One of the most interesting and least threatening ways to introduce more women's writing into the curriculum is to pair books —one by a woman, one by a man—so that the differing points of view can be compared to see if gender makes a difference. A future NCTE project might be to publish a list of women's literature that has been taught and proved to be worthy as literature. (An extensive reference list of anthologies, commentaries, and contacts for more references are appended.)

Chew, Charles, ed.; and others. "Reader Response in the Classroom." New York State English Council. 1986. 134 p. [ED 277 019]

   Focusing on reader response in the classroom, the works collected in this book represent the results of a five-week summer institute in which 25 middle-school, high-school, and college teachers studied the principles and applications of literature instruction. The following essays are included: an introduction by G. Garber; "An Overview of the Method" (P. Hansbury); "Reader Response: Theory and Practice" (P. Hansbury); "Formalist Criticism in the Secondary Classroom" (R. DeFabio); "A Formalist Lesson Plan for Salinger's 'A Perfect Day for Bananafish' Used with Advanced Seventh Grades" (M. McKay); "A Formalist Lesson: 'The Death of the Ball Turret Gunner'" (C. Forman); "Introduction to Historical/Cultural Methods of Literary Inquiry and Instruction" (M. Kelley); "An Historical-Cultural Approach to 'The Whole Town's Sleeping'" (J. Butterfield); "Introduction to Psychological Criticism" (B. A. Boyce); "A Psychoanalytic Approach to Joseph Conrad's 'The Secret Sharer'" (G. B. Kamm); "A Psychological Critic Looks at 'A Narrow Fellow in the Grass'" (D. J. Marhafer); "Overview of Mythological Criticism" (D. M. Quick); "The Application of Archetypal Criticism to John Knowles 'A Separate Peace'" (D. M. Quick); "A Feminist Archetypal Approach to 'Jane Eyre'" (R. Y. DeFabio); "Multiple Critical Approaches to 'A Rose for Emily'" (C. Reynolds); "Multiple Critical Approaches to 'One Flew Over the Cuckoo's Nest'" (C. Forman); and "Yes, But Does It Work?" (D. M. Quick).

Connolly, Ann. "Taking the Fear Away from Learning: Observations of Contemporary Fiction Taught by Carol Johnson at the Chestnut Hill School in a City in New York." Report Series 2.3. Center for the Learning and Teaching of Literature, School of Education, 1400 Washington Ave., ED B-9, University at Albany, State University of New York, Albany, NY 12222. 1989. 26 p. [ED 315 757]

One of a series of six portraits of high-school literature classrooms, this paper contains a detailed, evocative characterization of how one master teacher introduced, undertook, and guided the study of literature, focusing in particular on how the teacher interacted with students in the context of discussion of a literary work in class. Tells how a teacher-researcher observed an instructional unit of literature by (1) conducting taped interviews with the teacher as well as with her students; (2) gathering lesson plans, study guidelines, and assignments related to the instructional units to be observed; and (3) making videotapes of the classes involved; and finally (4) writing a narrative account of what had been observed in the class and what its significance appeared to be. This account describes a class of 12 seniors at a private academy for girls reading Margaret Craven's "I Heard the Owl Call My Name," and led by their teacher to make personal connections with literature, to express and maintain their beliefs while allowing others their opinions—how in short, they are coming to view literature as one of life's amenities.

Cunneen, Sheila. "Earthseans and Earthteens," *English Journal,* v74 n2 p68-69 Feb 1985.

> Explains the attraction of Ursula LeGuin's "A Wizard of Earthsea" for teenage readers by showing how many of its themes reflect the concerns of adolescent life.

Curran, Stuart. "Altering the 'I': Women Poets and Romanticism," *ADE Bulletin,* n88 p9-12 Win 1988.

> Notes that although women were prominent in the English world of letters in the late 1700s, eighteenth-century women writers have been ignored by literary scholars and historians. Asserts that this discrimination in favor of the canonized Romantics, such as Blake and Wordsworth, excludes women Romantics' valuable and lively literary contributions.

Davis, Ellen; and Solar, Judith. "Gizzard Soup Made with Love: Teaching Anne Tyler's *Dinner at the Homesick Restaurant,*" *Exercise Exchange,* v29 n1 p36-39 Fall 1983.

> Presents a teaching guide for the novel *Dinner at the Homesick Restaurant,* including questions for discussion and writing about individual characters and the novel as a whole.

Folsom, Marcia McClintock. "Gallant Red Brick and Plain China: Teaching 'A Room of One's Own.'" *College English,* v45 n3 p254-62 Mar 1983.

> Describes how a teacher taught a book by Virginia Woolf at the beginning of a course in women's literature so that it could serve as a touchstone for later reading and writing.

Gilbert, Sandra M. "Teaching Plath's 'Daddy' to Speak to Undergraduates." *ADE Bulletin,* n76 p38-42 Win 1983.

> Offers suggestions for putting Sylvia Plath's poem "Daddy" together with its context, canon, and composition to introduce students effectively to Plath's intelligence and aesthetic energy.

Goldstein, Janet Mendell. "From Pandora to Nora: Literature and Women's Liberation." Paper presented at the Annual Meeting of the National Council of Teachers of English, 1973. 11 p. [ED 088 099]

> Describes a ten-week elective course for high-school seniors, entitled "Literature and Women's Liberation." The purposes of the course were (1) to introduce students to some of the classic fictional, nonfictional, poetic, and dramatic statements concerning the role of women, as well as to quite a few recent commentaries on this theme; and (2) to raise the students' consciousness concerning the very real

problems that have confronted women throughout their struggle for independence and identity. In addition, materials from newspapers, magazines, photographs, and advertisements were used. The class began with an introduction to some of the great authors of the Western literary tradition who hated women and moved toward a study of traditional stereotypes of women in contemporary society. Mass media and guest speakers added variety to the lessons. Student response to the class was enthusiastic.

Hall, Kristen. "The Fig Tree's Lessons," *Humanities,* v9 n5 p22-23 Sep-Oct 1988.

Describes the dramatization of Katherine Anne Porter's story, "The Fig Tree's Lessons." Discusses the process by which this story was made accessible to an audience of 8-to-12-year-old children. Notes that this program attempts to avoid simplification of the profound human experience of dealing with death.

Harris, Raymond. *Best Short Stories. Middle Level. 10 Stories for Young Adults—with Lessons for Teaching the Basic Elements of Literature.* 1983. 463 p. [ED 301 874]

This workbook contains ten short stories by modern masters aimed at young adult readers, with each story followed by a concise lesson on a basic element of literature (such as plot, setting, or mood) clearly illustrated in the story. Some of the authors represented in the book are John Updike, Isaac Bashevis Singer, Carson McCullers, and Ray Bradbury. Practice exercises demonstrating the element of literature discussed, multiple-choice comprehension questions, discussion guides, and writing exercises follow each story. Answer keys and charts to record progress in comprehension are appended.

Jennings, Maude M. "How It All Began: Sour Grapes," *Feminist Teacher,* v5 n2 p16-19 Fall 1990.

Presents a one-act play by the author, using Eula Lee (the feminist author's alter ego) as a storyteller. Embellishes upon the sour-grapes fable to teach good sportsmanship and what "sour grapes" means. Enacts the author's ideas about teaching cultural values through storytelling.

Jennings, Maude M.; and others. "Tell Them a Story," *Feminist Teacher,* v5 n2 p15 Fall 1990.

Introduces the work of Eula Lee, a fictional storyteller and the feminist author's alter ego. Encourages teachers at all educational levels to become storytellers for the magic of the story itself, the instructional strength of metaphor, and the personal power of interpretation and presentation. Stresses the stories' abilities to reinforce community values and involve students.

Jensen, Marvin D. "Teaching Interpersonal Communication through Novels, Plays, and Films." 1981. 17 p. [ED 213 055]

> Intended for use by instructors of college-level interpersonal communication courses, this paper offers examples of theoretical concepts of interpersonal communication that can be illustrated through literature and popular film. The first part of the paper discusses the criteria on which the selection of novels, plays, and films for the study of human interaction should be based. It then applies Abraham Maslow's five characteristics of the self-actualized person to the central character in the novel *A Separate Peace.* The third part of the paper examines the theories of C. Hampden-Turner and V. Frankl as they are illustrated in the writing of author Willa Cather, while the fourth part applies the theories of psychiatrist R. D. Laing to the play *Equus.* The fifth part discusses psychiatrist Thomas Szasz's theories as they are explored in the play *Whose Life Is It Anyway?* and applies the rational-emotive process described by Albert Ellis to the behavior in the novel and film *Ordinary People.* The final section of the paper examines the film *Midnight Express* as being of little value in the study of human relationships, because it distorts the reality portrayed in the original book.

Jiji, Vera, ed. "A Sourcebook of Interdisciplinary Materials in American Drama: George Aiken, 'Uncle Tom's Cabin' (1852). Showcasing American Drama." 1983. 46 p. [ED 236 724]

> Prepared as part of a project aimed at redressing the neglect of American drama in college and secondary-school programs of drama, American literature, and American studies, this booklet provides primary and secondary source materials to assist teachers and students in the study of George L. Aiken's dramatic adaptation of Harriet Beecher Stowe's *Uncle Tom's Cabin.* Materials in the first part of the booklet deal with literary and theatrical considerations of (1) the popular sentiments of the novel and play, (2) Tom as the Black maternal Christ, (3) nineteenth-century staging of the play, (4) the play as melodrama, (5) the play as drama, and (6) a variant version of the auction scene. Materials in the second section cover cultural, social, and historical considerations and place the play in an historical perspective; provide a case against it; and offer a view of a similar play, *The Escape or a Leap for Freedom,* by William Wells Brown. The third section contains selections from primary source materials, including critical commentary on the validity of the picture of slavery offered in the play and novel. Questions for study are included in the appendixes.

Kamholtz, Jonathan Z.; Sheets, Robin A. "Women Writers and the Survey of English Literature: A Proposal and Annotated Bibliography for Teachers," *College English,* v46 n3 p278-300 Mar 1984.

> Suggests names of women writers as alternatives to traditionally taught male writers, identifies women writers as representatives of a parallel tradition and genres not usually studied in a survey, and discusses some of the best feminist scholarship and criticism.

Kelly, Patricia. "Women's Studies in the English Class," *English Journal,* v74 n3 p88-90 Mar 1985.

> Reviews new publications in women's studies and suggests applications for use in the English class.

Klinkenborg, Kay F. "A Selected Bibliography for Integrating Women's Studies into the College Curriculum," *Feminist Teacher,* v4 n1 p26-31 Spr 1989.

> Provides selected references to help college teachers integrate women's studies into the college curriculum; gives examples of integration projects along with methodologies. Offers resources for integration into the liberal-arts curriculum but does not include references for integration into specific academic disciplines.

Lee, Valerie. "Strategies for Teaching Black Women's Literature in a White Cultural Context," *Sage: A Scholarly Journal on Black Women,* v6 n1 p74-76 Sum 1989.

> Describes strategies used in teaching Black women's studies courses to predominantly White classes at Denison University. Provides suggestions on the selection and sequence of texts, especially novels, that merge Black and female concerns and promote exploration of the issues of race, gender, and class.

Maier, Carol. "Teaching about Women in Hispanic Literature: Current Methods and Materials." Paper presented at the Annual Meeting of the Modern Language Association, 1979. 8 p. [ED 194 242]

> Awareness of a new and altered method of teaching literature, similar to that described by Adrienne Rich, grew from the experience of teaching a small introductory course in twentieth-century Hispanic women writers to students with diverse language, cultural, and economic backgrounds. Although about half the students were native Spanish speakers, the material seemed foreign to them. As is often the case with women's-studies classes, the works read were also "antihierarchical," or outside the usual support system of back-up material; therefore, student response and discussion were minimal until

after the instructor attempted to relate the material and weave a context for it as she saw fit. The particulars of each writer appeared unimportant until the students could detect individual voices among the writers. Returning to, and rereading texts, in order to compare the authors and their different uses of similar situations and themes, gave the students the chance to discern a "female voice" in contemporary Hispanic literature.

Mandel, Barrett J. "Literature Is Its Audience," *College Teaching*, v35 n3 p107-10 Sum 1987.

    Three elements of the reading process—presence, mediation, and ego response—help students discover their own ontological, intellectual, and psychological role in bringing forth literature's meanings. Students experience a dramatic shift in their ability to make sense of literature as they become increasingly conscious of these three elements.

Matthews, Dorothy, ed. "Writing Assignments Based on Literary Works," Illinois *English Bulletin*, v72 n3 Spr 1985. [ED 255 923]

    The literature selections serving as the basis for writing assignments in the articles in this journal issue range from time-honored English classics (*Beowulf, Sir Gawain and the Green Knight*) and American standards (*A Farewell to Arms, The Scarlet Letter*) to contemporary fiction. The articles deal with works by women writers (Shirley Jackson, Caroline Gordon, Willa Cather, Kate Chopin, and Toni Bambara) and works especially suited for both high school (Lee's *To Kill a Mockingbird*) and college study (Coover's *The Babysitter*). The assignments in the articles call not only for critical analysis but also for responding in journals, imaginative rewriting, imitating style, and using writing as a reading strategy. Some assignments in the articles ask for student response and imaginative projection, whereas others demand a rigorous examination of the text, with writing leading to a better understanding of the work as literature.

Mayer, Sister J. Eleanor. "Neighborhoods: Maya Angelou's 'Harlem Hopscotch' (Modern Poetry in the Classroom)," *English Journal*, v77 n5 p86-88 Sep 1988.

    Recounts the experience of analyzing Maya Angelou's poem "Harlem Hopscotch," and how it helped students see the extended metaphor and the parallels to life experiences.

Meerson, Mary Lou. "Integrating the Language Arts: Alternatives and Strategies Using Trade Books as Models for Student Writing." Paper presented at the Annual Meeting of the International Reading Association, 1988. 8 p. [ED 294 210]

Although teachers are often told to use literature as models for students' writing, they are rarely provided with specific suggestions on how, when, and why to use literature, or trade books, in their curriculum. There are many situations in which the use of literature can be helpful to the novice writer. With pre-kindergarten or kindergarten children, teachers can help students build schemas by writing books themselves. This type of schema-building continues at all levels, and is assisted by books about books, such as *Harold and the Purple Crayon* and *Simon's Book*. The technique of "copy change," using a story as the basis for writing a similar story, helps students develop their personal voice, and can be used at any level. For older students who are less confident of their writing ability, books such as *How to Write Secret Codes* and *How to Draw Cartoons* are effective in easing their anxiety by providing "how to" practice. Other suggestions for employing literature as a model for student writing include using trade books to teach literary devices (*The Diary of Anne Frank* for diaries, and *Science Experiments You Can Eat* for content-area writing) and writing book extensions (prologues or epilogues for books, new stories for well-known characters, or changing the setting of a story). An annotated bibliography of trade books is appended.

Moore, Lisa. "One-on-One: Pairing Male and Female Writers." *English Journal,* v78 n6 p34-38 Oct 1989.

Describes an approach that pairs every male-authored novel, play, short story, or poem taught in the English curriculum with one written by a woman. Illustrates this approach in a course pairing Emily Dickinson and Walt Whitman. Provides an annotated list of works in which the subject of gender issues in schools is examined.

Morgan, Alice. "On Teaching *Emma,*" *Journal of General Education,* v24 n2 1972.

Author points out two major difficulties with *Emma* as an assignment: information (social facts, physical facts) needed to understand the setting and events, and the problem of making possible some relationship with so unreforming a work.

Neier, Sue, ed. "Novels & Adolescent Fiction." *The Idea Factory*, Win-Spr 1985. [ED 266 484]

The teaching activities presented in this issue are intended to enhance literature instruction for students in grades 5-9. The activities include those specifically designed for use with *The Diary of Anne Frank, Johnny Tremain, The Contender, No Promises in the Wind,* and *Fahrenheit 451.* The journal also contains general activities centered around reading strategies, book reports, searching for identity, group discussions, characterization, point of view, use of popular music or poetry, and creating students' own books.

Parker, Barbara. *Nonsexist Curriculum Development: Theory into Practice. The Handbook of the Curriculum Design Project at the University of Colorado, Boulder.* 1984. 132 p. [ED 286 773]

    Addressing the problems of access and time constraints, this curriculum guide describes a core undergraduate women's-studies course in which college-level students learn to research, prepare, and present nonsexist curriculum units for public-school classrooms. The course was designed to (1) compensate for the lack of information in the traditional curriculum about women in culture and society; (2) correct any sexism and misinformation generated by traditional disciplines; and (3) equip students to contribute new research and knowledge in the field of women's studies. Containing information on how to recruit teachers and course participants, this document also includes instructional packets that focus on teaching units for elementary, middle, and junior/senior high-school students. Tests used to evaluate course participants' gender biases, a course syllabus, and student assignments are included. Stressing the educational objectives of content, skills, and experience, the course lectures focus on (1) assumptions about males and females, (2) the socialization process, (3) videotaping, (4) sources of information, (5) school socialization, (6) bias in language, and (7) sexism and other "isms" in educational curriculums. Sample testing, course evaluation instruments, examples of various grade-level curriculum units, and an annotated bibliography are featured; charts and graphs are included.

Peck, David. *Novels of Initiation: A Guidebook for Teaching Literature to Adolescents.* 1989. 193 p. [ED 306 584]

    Intended as a guidebook for high-school English teachers, this book contains analyses of American novels commonly read in high-school English classes. Each chapter is divided into two sections: an analysis of the novel, including discussions of story and setting, characters, themes, and language and style; and a guide to teaching the novel in the classroom, containing suggestions for approaching the novel, writing and discussion topics, and bridges to related literary works. Two appendices provide sample thematic units, with listings of appropriate titles, and a selective list of other American novels of initiation. A glossary lists literary terms discussed throughout the book. Novels covered in the book are (1) *The Catcher in the Rye* (J. D. Salinger); (2) *Adventures of Huckleberry Finn* (Mark Twain); (3) *The Chocolate War* (Robert Cormier); (4) *Ordinary People* (Judith Guest); (5) *The Bell Jar* (Sylvia Plath); (6) *The*

Great Gatsby (F. Scott Fitzgerald); (7) *The Red Badge of Courage* (Stephen Crane); (8) *To Kill a Mockingbird* (Harper Lee); (9) *Member of the Wedding* (Carson McCullers); (10) *The Red Pony* (John Steinbeck); (11) *A Day No Pigs Would Die* (Robert Newton Peck); and (12) *Roll of Thunder, Hear My Cry* (Mildred D. Taylor).

Pondrom, Cyrena N. "Gender and the (Re)Formation of the Canon: Is Politics All?" *ADE Bulletin,* n91 p21-28 Win 1988.

Argues that literary history and estimations of literary value are inseparable, and that their connection has import for debate on the contents of the literary canon. Suggests possible requirements for developing a feminist theory and practice of evaluation.

Ritchie, Joy S. "Confronting the 'Essential' Problem: Reconnecting Feminist Theory and Pedagogy," *Journal of Advanced Composition,* v10 n2 p249-73 Fall 1990.

Describes an undergraduate women's literature course in which students write in journals. Argues that the course may resolve conflict between feminist teachers, who dislike some theorists' uncritical view of feminism, and theorists, who dislike the taint of male philosophy in feminist teaching. Suggests that course interaction can bridge these views.

Rosowski, Susan J. "Discovering Symbolic Meaning: Teaching with Willa Cather," *English Journal,* v71 n8 p14-17 Dec 1982.

Suggests that the works of Willa Cather can be used to introduce students to the skills and outlooks needed to read literature.

Schaars, Mary Jo. "Teaching *My Antonia,* with Guidance from Rosenblatt," *English Journal,* v77 n1 p54-58 Jan 1988.

Presents a student-guided approach (based on Louise M. Rosenblatt's "Literature as Exploration") to teaching Willa Cather's *My Antonia.*

Sessa, Anne Dzamba, ed. *Sisterhood Surveyed.* Proceedings of the Mid-Atlantic Women's Studies Association Conference, 1982. Women's Studies Office, West Chester, West Chester University, West Chester, Pennsylvania. 121 p. [ED 239 567]

Proceedings of the 1982 conference of the Mid-Atlantic Women's Studies Association are presented. Synopses of sessions include the following topics: iconography of sisterhood, matriarchy, ethnic and cultural critiques, political perspectives, and nontraditional women students. Conference papers and authors are as follows: "Friends for Half a Century: The Relationship of Charlotte Perkins Gilman and Grace

Channing Stetson" (Ann J. Lane); "Cygnets and Ducklings: George Eliot and the Problem of Female Community" (Linda Hunt); "Harmonious Sisters, Voice and Verse: Women and Fiction in Milton's Early Verse" (Janet E. Halley); "Women and the Scottish Enlightenment" (Esther L. Barazzone); "The Education of Germaine de Stael, or Rousseau Betrayed" (Madelyn Gutwirth); "Loyalty and Betrayal: Iseut and Brangien in the Tristan Romances of Beroul and Thomas" (Roberta L. Kreuger); "Communities of Sisters: Utopian Fiction by U.S. Women, 1970-1980" (Carol F. Kessler); "Rosa Mayreder (1858-1938), Pioneer of Austrian Feminism" (Mary-Ann Reiss); "Feminism as a Sophisticated Concept: Good News, Bad News, and Old News" (Sylvan H. Cohen); "Feminist Issues and Feminist Attitudes: Teaching Today's Students" (Paula S. Rothenberg); and "Changes in the Way Men and Women View Themselves and Each Other" (John Gormly, Anne Gormly).

Snow, Nancy Hill. "A Study of Point of View and Character in Preparation for Oral Performance of Cuttings from *The Optimist's Daughter*." Paper presented at the Annual Meeting of the Speech Communication Association, 1985. 18 p. [ED 269 832]

In the process of perfecting oral performances of selected scenes from Eudora Welty's *The Optimist's Daughter,* it is important to study point of view and character as they pertain to the play. Four aspects should be considered to understand the point of view: (1) the character's story, (2) the position from which the narrator speaks, (3) the channels used to convey information, and (4) the distance at which the narrator places the reader. In *The Optimist's Daughter,* the narrator is omniscient concerning the character of Laurel, and her position is that of an onlooker. Because the narrator explores Laurel's thoughts and feelings, the reader is near Laurel, the story, and the narrator. Among the criteria to be considered in character analysis are physical, social, and dispositional characteristics. Readers analyzing the characters of Laurel and Fay, her stepmother, discover many differences in their characters, including being opposite in physical appearance, social background, and personality. Because Eudora Welty has vividly portrayed the characters in the play and has clearly presented the story from Laurel's point of view, an examination of character and point of view can give performers a foundation on which to build a satisfying presentation of *The Optimist's Daughter.*

Spacks, Patricia Meyer. "Emma's Happiness," *ADE Bulletin,* n84 p16-18 Fall 1986.

Discusses teaching J. Austen's *Emma* in light of the issue of happiness in order to make the novel more interesting to students who do not like Emma, the character. Suggests that the multiplicity of questions raised by Austen will provide sufficient material for discussion.

Stanton, Patricia A. "Women in Modern Indian Literature: High School Level." 1990. 28 p. [ED 325 433]

Secondary-school lessons on women in modern Indian society as they are portrayed in 20th century works of literature are presented. The lessons focus on four novels, and could be read in conjunction with the study of a period of Indian history. Each lesson features background on the author, a list of discussion questions, and suggested writing activities. An annotated list of works featuring 20th-century women authors who have been recognized by the world community for their achievements also is provided. As background reading for teachers, a lecture on the status of women and a brief history of the womens' movement in India is appended.

"Stories to Be Read Aloud (Booksearch)," *English Journal,* v78 n2 p87-90 Feb 1989.

Presents junior- and senior-high school teachers' suggestions for short stories to read aloud in a single class period, including "The Laughing Man" (J. D. Salinger), "A & P" (John Updike), "Epicac" (Kurt Vonnegut), "The Story of an Hour" (Kate Chopin), and "The Yellow Wallpaper" (Charlotte Perkins Gilman).

Styer, Sandra. "Integrating Women's Studies in Teacher Education: Some Recommended Strategies." 1983. 10 p. [ED 233 995]

The feasibility of incorporating women's studies into the regular teacher education curriculum was explored. Suggestions and recommendations on developing the curriculum were made, focusing on considerations such as (1) availability of adequate resource materials, (2) development of sample course syllabuses for instructors of women's studies in teacher education, (3) possible teaching strategies, such as cross-listing courses and team teaching, (4) degree to which women's studies have already been included in teacher education, (5) faculty members who would be willing to serve as resource persons in education classes, and (6) developmental possibilities inherent in seminars and study/discussion group sessions.

Summerfield, Geoffrey, and Judith Summerfield. *Reading(s).* 1989. 448 p. [ED 305 622]

Developed for college English courses, this book presents selections of poetry, short stories, and commentary intended to invite different ways of reading and interpreting literature. An introduction provides an overview of the book's content, as well as a discussion of how to read. The first section, "Entering a Language," is about the development of a reader, the variety of worlds that can be entered through reading, and how these other worlds modify readers' relationships to their own world. The second section, "Losing Nature? Gaining Culture?" concerns the relationship between nature and culture, and how one learns to "read" these two interacting, often opposing, worlds. The theme of the third section, "Negotiations and Renegotiations," focuses on how people negotiate the relationship between their culture and its values, with other cultures, and with people who may represent values different from the reader's values. Each text begins with a brief introduction, followed by the text itself, then a presentation of the key features and issues that the text offers. In addition, occasional brief commentaries are included on important aspects of reading and of the particular "reading," and most of the texts are followed by suggestions for discussion and reflection. Suggestions for various writing prompts are offered at the end of each chapter. Some of the selections included in this book are "Captain Murder" (Charles Dickens); "In the Fig Tree I Learned to Read" (Lillian Hellman); "Through the Eyes of Men" (Simone de Beauvoir); "Autobiographical Notes" (James Baldwin); "Fifteen" (William Stafford); "The First Day of School" (Cynthia Ozick); "Sunrise" (Eudora Welty); "Memories of Waves" (Walt Whitman); "I Know Green Apples" (Mark Twain); "Song of the Hen's Head" (Margaret Atwood); "Down by the Salley Gardens" (W. B. Yeats); "On Reading Fiction" (Philip Roth); and "Stranger on a Train" (Virginia Woolf).

Valentine, K. B. *Twenty Questions to the Puzzle of Meaning in Literature for the Oral Interpreter.* 1975. 50 p. [ED 120 870]

In order to help students in oral interpretation or English classes comprehend the literature they read, this document outlines a question-answer-rehearse procedure that resolves the paradox of understanding before they perform a text. The twenty questions, formulated to provide a solid foundation for later explication and deeper study, are stated briefly for teacher overview. In the section written to students, the questions are restated in complete form with suggested explanations for each question. The document concludes with a glossary of literary terms and an analysis of a poem by Emily Dickinson using these twenty questions.

Wagner, Linda W. "Teaching 'The Bluest Eye.'" *ADE Bulletin,* n83 p28-31 Spr 1986.

Shows how teaching "The Bluest Eye" not only helps students learn about the time period of the novel and its relevant issues and techniques but also helps them to understand themselves. Shows how it can fit into contemporary literature classes, introductory courses to fiction or literature, or into women's literature classes.

Walkington, J. W. "Women and Power in Henrik Ibsen and Adrienne Rich," *English Journal,* v80 n3 p64-68 Mar 1991.

Shares how one teacher of world literature used the writings of Henrik Ibsen and Adrienne Rich to help students come to a full understanding of the creation of gender stereotypes and investigate the world around them.

Waxman, Barbara Frey. "Politics of the Survey Course: Feminist Challenges," *Teaching English in the Two Year College,* v16 n1 p17-22 Feb 1989.

Argues that survey courses can teach students about values underlying syllabuses and show that literary interpretations are political. Suggests four ways to change the survey course syllabus, and discusses the effects of these changes on classroom discussions. Emphasizes the need to undermine the patriarchal authority of the traditional literary canon.

Weston, Ruth D. "Eudora Welty as a Resource for the Writing Classroom." 1990. [ED 321 279]

In addition to her work as novelist and critic, Eudora Welty is also a valuable resource for the teaching of composition through both her theory and example, for she is always writing about writing. Many of Welty's essays on literary theory speak to problems encountered in the college writing class. Perhaps the most accessible text for demonstrating Welty as a writing teacher is her autobiography, *One Writer's Beginnings,* in which each section deals with a problem basic to all writing and lends itself to student writing experience. In the first section, entitled "Listening," Welty's dynamic and expressive verbs and adjectives are the basis for an exercise in diction. Classroom assignments emphasizing concrete, concise language and character analysis grow out of this section when used in conjunction with the Welty essay entitled "Clamorous to Learn." Also, Welty's own readings of writers she admires give insights into insightful listening, helping students make meaning emerge from texts before responding in their own writing. In the section entitled "Learning To See," Welty's text provides a model of her visual imagination as well as evidence of her belief in the importance of what she calls writing with an "eye for the telling detail." The last section, "Finding a Voice," addresses the techniques of focusing, illustrated in one of her early stories. It includes a discussion of a writer's efforts at achieving distance, perspective, and frame of vision. An appendix contains student writing assignments for "Finding a Voice."

Whelchel, Marianne. "Transforming the Canon with Nontraditional Literature by Women," *College English,* v46 n6 p587-97 Oct 1984.

>Suggests and describes nontraditional women's literature appropriate for inclusion in English courses; shows how it fills curricular gaps in terms of the voices and experiences it makes available. Also describes the experience of teaching one such text, *The Maimie Papers,* and explores how students can uncover important material and become sophisticated readers through original projects.

Williams, Michael. "Teaching the 'A' Level Text: Alice Walker—*The Color Purple,*" *Use of English,* v40 n2 p45-55 Spr 1989.

>Examines Alice Walker's novel, *The Color Purple.* Describes secondary school students' reactions to, and explorations of, the novel.

Worsley, Dale; Mayer, Bernadette. *The Art of Science Writing.* Teachers and Writers Collaborative, 5 Union Square West, New York, New York 10003. 1989. 218 p. [ED 304 702]

>Aimed at secondary-school science and English teachers, this book presents practical advice for developing good student writing in science and mathematics. Five main sections cover (1) an essay-development workshop, (2) 47 specific writing assignments, (3) over 30 questions teachers ask about science writing and the answers, (4) an anthology of 43 selections of science writing from Shakespeare, Darwin, Freud, Carl Sagan, Rachel Carson, and others, and (5) an annotated bibliography of over 150 books useful for the teaching of science writing. An appendix by Russel W. Kenyon discusses teaching math writing.

Designed by teachers... for teachers

E ach volume contains alternatives to textbook teaching. The acronym TRIED reflects the reliability of these hands-on, how-to instructional designs: Ideas that have been tried and tested by other teachers, reported in the ERIC database, and now redesigned to be teacher-easy and student-friendly.

> "As educators return to their classrooms for a new year of experiences and challenges..., how many teachers have the time to seek out fresh, effective lesson ideas, especially during the start of a busy new school year? the TRIED series can help.... The TRIED series is a valuable yet reasonably priced addition to any teaching repertoire."
>
> —*WSRA Journal*

Choose from these 13 Titles in the TRIED Series:

Teaching Literature Written by Women
Expands literature-based learning to include important works of 29 women. Strategies develop respect for gender equity and teach the novels, stories, and poems of Madeline L'Engle, Maya Angelou, Anne Frank, and other women of the past and present. (Elem/Mid/Sec)   T14; $16.95

Teaching Values through Teaching Literature
Presents teaching strategies for today's most powerful instructional materials, including novels, folk literature, poetry, and ethnic literature. Features a section on setting up a program in values clarification through literature. (Mid/Sec)   T13; $16.95

Reading and Writing across the High School Science and Math Curriculum
Contains exciting reading and writing alternatives to the textbook approach. Explore lessons on "writing to learn" in math and science: Journal writing, scientific poetry writing, and using writing to overcome those dreaded "story problems." (Sec)   T12; $16.95

Celebrate Literacy! The Joy of Reading and Writing
Covers the full range of language-arts skills and literature to turn your elementary school into a reading and writing carnival including literacy slumber parties, book birthdays, and battles of the books. (Elem)   T11; $14.95

Working with Special Students in English/Language Arts
Helps take the worry out of teaching special students. Strategies to organize your classroom; use computers; implement cooperative learning; and teach thinking skills, reading, and writing to students with special needs. (Elem/Mid/Sec)   T10; $14.95

A High School Student's Bill of Rights
Invites middle and high school students to explore the U.S. Constitution and other bodies of law. Lesson approaches are focused on precedent-setting legal cases that have dealt with student's rights when they were contested in the school context. May be used as a whole course, a mini-course, or as supplementary activities. (Mid/Sec)   T09; $14.95

Reading Strategies for the Primary Grades
Presents a storehouse of clever ideas to begin reading and writing, and to build vocabulary and comprehension. Use stories, poems, response logs, oral reading, Whole Language, and much more! (Elem)   T08; $14.95

Language Arts for Gifted Middle School Students
Supplies challenging lessons in a variety of language-arts areas; communication skills, literature, mass media, theater arts, reading, writing. Activities designed for gifted students also work for others. (Mid)   T07; $14.95

Remedial Reading for Elementary School Students
Uses games and reading activities to stimulate imagination, develop reading skills, and strengthen comprehension. (Elem)   T05; $14.95

Writing Exercises for High School Students
Motivates students to explore creative, and expository writing. Introduces the young writer to all the basics of good writing. (Sec)   T04; $14.95

Critical Thinking, Reading, and Writing
Encourages reading, writing, and thinking in a critically reflective, inventive way for students at all levels. Practical classroom activities make critical thinking an achievable goal. (Elem/Mid/Sec)   T03; $14.95

Teaching the Novel
Offers strategies for teaching many novels, including *To Kill a Mockingbird, The Color Purple, The Scarlet Letter,* and other oft-taught works of interest to middle school and high school students. (Mid/Sec)   T02; $14.95

Writing across the Social Studies Curriculum
Provides examples of how to connect writing activities with lessons on important topics in the social studies—a writing across the curriculum approach. (Mid/Sec)   T01; $14.95

To order, mail check or purchase order to: ERIC/EDINFO Press • Indiana University • P.O. Box 5953 • Bloomington, IN 47407
Phone 1 (800) 925-7853 • Fax (812) 331-2776 • Please add 10% for shipping and handling, minimum $3.00.